ILLUSTRATORS
ANNUAL **2015**

Jury 2015

BENJAMIN CHAUD

SVJETLAN JUNAKOVIĆ

CHARLES KIM

PAOLA PARAZZOLI

ULLA RHEDIN

An event by:

MILAN 2015

Official Partner

President
DUCCIO CAMPAGNOLI

Sales & Marketing Director
ALDO SANSONE

Exhibition Director
MARCO MOMOLI

Group Product Manager
ELENA PASOLI

Exhibition Manager
ROBERTA CHINNI

Bologna Children's Book Fair
Show Office
DEANNA BELLUTI
CRISTINA PANCALDI

Illustrators Exhibition
BEATRICE MONETTI
RUNA BIGNAMI

Bologna Children's Book Fair
Piazza Costituzione, 6
40128 Bologna, Italy
www.bolognachildrensbookfair.com
bookfair@bolognafiere.it

ILLUSTRATORS
ANNUAL **2015**

CONTENTS

Does your creative process involve a certain routine, or do your illustrations come about differently each time?

There is a different process each time. Something unusual is desirable, always, something chaotic, in order for the poetic flow to occur. I do not generally follow any routine in my work, but I understand that even some routine can be important to corrupt stillness. Artistic creation is about contradiction. Certain characters and images only actually start to exist from the moment in which you can count on the unexpected.

What is the difference between illustration and narration for you? There is no difference. Illustration is narration. Words are images. Each image tells a story, even an abstract image. From the moment in which the image connects with the reader, transmitting a certain sensation, memory, association, (even an abstract idea of blue or yellow, a pure shape or a more descriptive drawing), the image brings challenge, brings narration. Words are images, images are words.

How do text and image communicate in an illustrated book?

There are two key words here: *text* and *imagination*. Two words which explain and define this relationship. Imagination comes from *image* - and so fiction comes from there. It is not really the case that one concept takes precedence over the other, there is dialogue between them both. The same goes for text. When we talk about text we need to remember that the image is also text. The word *text* comes from *texture*, literally, something that is woven. The word plot also has similar roots. This word is also linked to textile. Therefore the word *text* and the word *imagination* are deeply linked, text turning into images and images turning into text.

Could you give us some reference to something that has influenced your visual style?

I was born in Brasilia, the capital of Brazil, and I grew up under the military dictatorship, which was a regime of exclusion, of suppression of thought. Brasilia was designed by architects, illustrators, designers, educators, free thinking people with a philosophy of inclusion, who had an idea of creating an ideal city, a utopia. But many of these people were displaced, exiled or imprisoned because of the military regime. It was a time when people could be tortured or killed just because

Following a consolidated tradition, as the Hans Christian Andersen winner, Roger Mello is the author of the cover of the 2015 Annual Illustrators Catalogue for the Bologna Children's Book Fair, where he will also have a personal exhibition of 24 of his artworks.

Born in Brasilia in 1965, ROGER MELLO has illustrated more than one hundred titles, 22 of which he also authored. An ESDI/UERJ industrial design graduate, Roger worked with the Brazilian designer Ziraldo. He has received countless awards in Brazil and abroad as both illustrator and writer, including Brazil's National Foundation of Books for Children and Young Adults' award. He was one of the five artists shortlisted in 2010 and 2012 for the International Hans Christian Andersen Award, which he subsequently won in 2014. Hans Christian Andersen Award, awarded by the International Board on Books for Young People (IBBY), is considered the Nobel Prize for children's literature and enjoys the patronage of Queen Margrethe II of Denmark. Roger has also won Brazil's acclaimed Jabuti Award some nine times. He has received lifetime achievement awards from the Brazilian Academy of Letters and the Brazilian Union of Writers. Roger has participated in many international book fairs held in Catalonia, Rome, Frankfurt, Bologna, Gothenburg, Brooklyn (Brooklyn Public Library), Sarmede (Le Immagini Della Fantasia), New Delhi, Padua (I Colori del Sacro), Nami Island (South Korea), Bogota, Santo Domingo, and Havana. His book *Meninos do Mangue* (Mangrove Kids) received the international best book of the year award from the Fondation Espace Enfants (Switzerland) in 2002. Together with other Brazilian authors, Roger was a guest of honour at the Brazil Hall of the 2005 Salon du Livre in Montreuil, France. In the same year his illustrations of a book of folk verses entitled Nau Catarineta were exhibited in Paris libraries. Three of his books (*The Flower on the Other Side*; *You Can't be Too Careful*, and *Mangrove Kids*) were included on the "list of books that every child should read before becoming an adult," published by Folha de São Paulo in 2007. His works were also included in the exhibition, curated by FNLIJ (Fundação Nacional do Livro Infantil e Juvenil), between November 2011 and February 2012 at the Internationale Jugendbibliothek, Blutenburg Castle - Munich, Germany. The same exhibition was part of a 2013 Internationale Jugendbibliothek itinerant exhibition to the German cities of Cologne and Wetzlar and then to the Chihiro Art Museum, Azumino (Japan) from May 16 to July 22, 2014. The show will go to the Tokyo Chihiro Art Museum in 2015. From January to April 2013, Roger's illustrations for his book *Jean fil à fil*, published in France by éditions MeMo, were shown in La Maison des Contes et des Histoires. His works were also included in the 2013 Year of Brazil exhibition at the Frankfurt Book Fair, organized by the National Library Foundation. In 2014 he was one of the guest authors at Sweden's Gothenburg Book Fair. Roger's books are published in France, Belgium, Switzerland, China, Korea, Japan, Sweden, Denmark, Argentina and Mexico. In November 2014, Roger also received the Chen Bochui International Children's Literature Award for the Best Foreign Author in China. In addition, the book illustrated by him - *A Feather* - was awarded the prize for the Most Beautiful Book in China. Roger's exhibition throughout September and October 2014 at the Seoul Arts Center in Korea was attended by an average number of 1300 people per day. Seoul's most prestigious newspaper hailed it as one of the 10 best exhibitions in Korea, a country that had also hosted shows of Munch and Van Gogh. Roger is the author of the plays *A Story of the Red Porpoise*, *Land of Mastodons*, *Curupira*, and *In Praise of Folly* (based on the book of the same name by Erasmus of Rotterdam), *Mangrove Kids* and *Entropia* (the last four staged at the Teatro III CCBB / RJ in 1996, 2003, 2005 and 2008 respectively). The play *Dispare*, both written and directed by him, was performed in 2011 at the Casa de Cultura Laura Alvim, and in 2012 at the Teatro Oi, Brasilia and in Montevideo, Uruguay (Teatro Solís). Roger also won the Coca-Cola Award for Children's Theatre (Best Text) with *A Story of the Red Porpoise*. The short movie *Cavalhadas Pirenópolis* (directed by Adolfo Lachtermacher based on the book by Roger) was selected for the Gramado Festival competition/exhibition (southern Brazil). The script of *The Mangrove Kids* (written in partnership with Adolfo Lachtermacher) was selected for the SESC Rio Script Laboratory for Cinema.

JARDINS, SOBRE POEMAS DE ROSEANA MURRAY (MANATI PUBLISHING HOUSE)

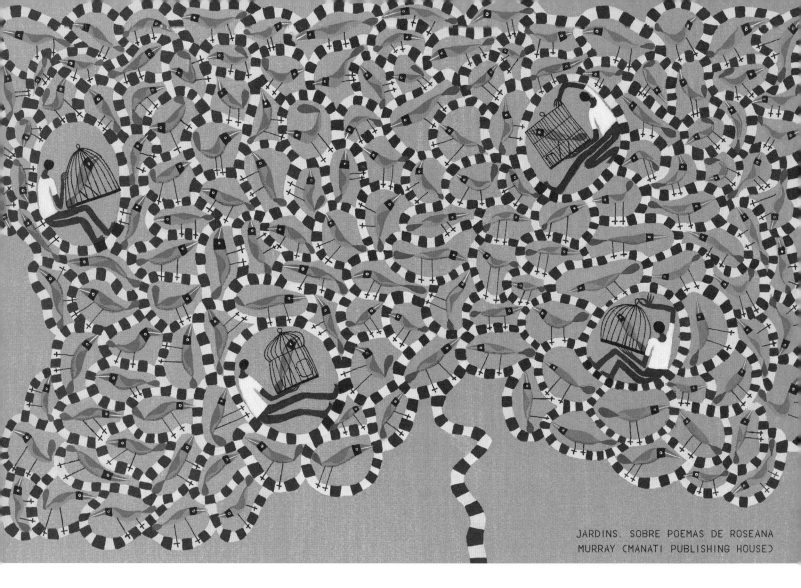

they had certain books that had been outlawed. This affected much of my training: understanding the book as such a powerful object, yet, at the same time, reading the ideology in form of visual poetry through images inside these creators' graphic projects all around the city. This is one of the factors that influenced the point of view of an entire generation.

What difference is there between being a book's illustrator and being its author?
I don't see a difference in this case either; the illustrator is an author. I see the book as a complete and indivisible object, a book is a whole. One aspect that has really influenced me was looking at artist's books, where only a few copies had been created. In terms of writing and illustrating, I am very influenced by numerous Brazilian authors as well as other foreign authors, such as Peter Bichsel or Harold Pinter. I work in theatre myself and use a playwright structure in my process with both the illustrations and the story.

As a children's illustrator, how important is it to know how to look at the world through a child's eyes?

I must confess that when I create a book, I do so rather selfishly, I do it for me. I think that is the best way to respect the reader. They can then decide for which age the book is intended. I think that the way to be most faithful to those who read is to not worry about this "child's eye". Otherwise we run the risk of creating a book for a reader who is so well defined that the book ends up not being meant for anybody at all. You cannot try to second-guess the reader's tastes. Trying to second-guess the reader means destroying the reader. My expectation is to see the free encounter between children and book. Circumstances may bring the book to the reader, but the reader can choose his or her book and then subvert the reading: I believe in this reader-author.

In what way has your training as a designer influenced your work as an illustrator?

The book is a single object, a dialogue between images and words, in which each part defines the other. The type, the space, the opening, the shape, the elements that make up the book are all connected to each other. This process, which goes from authors to bookbinders, to typographers means that the creation of the object-book involves a complex relationship, which also includes those working in publishing houses, people involved in the production of the book who turn it into a challenging object. So training as a designer is crucial in order to be able to conceive, beyond images and words, the shape of the book. From the proof to the final design. In a book, the images also interact as an open sequence, so, understanding this succession, understanding how text and image are woven together is important to be able to instigate all of the reader's senses. And then, it is the reader who subverts the book.

A WINDOW ON THE WORLD

THE ILLUSTRATORS EXHIBITION BETWEEN THE PRESENT AND THE FUTURE

The Illustrators Exhibition reaches its 49th edition, on the verge of next year's significant milestone which certainly ought to be celebrated. Over this past half-century, the Exhibition has become one of the most important occasions on an international level to present projects and debate illustration, as well as being a special place, a real agora for meetings between illustrators themselves. It is the history behind the previous editions that casts it in this role, making it an extraordinary event, much like the Children's Book Fair that organizes it. From publishers to illustrators, literary agents to authors, printers to packagers, translators to digital developers, booksellers to librarians: all of the players in an industry that – it bears repeating – in recent years, has once again demonstrated its vitality, remaining one of the few fixed points within the global publishing industry at a time of series and widespread difficulty. Among all of these, illustrators find a precise and unique point of reference at the Fair, embodying its most lively and vibrant aspect.

Since its first year in a now-distant 1967, the exhibition conferred a real cultural value to the Fair, turning it into an exciting place where ideas, opinions and visions could be exchanged. It was not only a marketplace where editors could show and sell their books, but also a place where you can learn from others. Moreover in a changing world images can serve as a mirror of what is transpiring. And this is why the Illustrators Exhibition is not just an integral part of the Fair, but its heart, a real window onto the world: it is here where thousands of images – this year, 15,000 works by almost 3000 illustrators from 62 different countries – are gathered, viewed and selected.

The specific stylistic features of different countries and cultures have become gradually less conspicuous over time. Communication, travel and the opportunity for exchange have made the world smaller and rendered the characteristics of the images themselves more alike. You now hear of the emergence of distinction not only in terms of cultural reference points, but also related to the personal stylistic choices of certain artists, whose influences transcend national borders and often makes them points of reference for many other illustrators. In recent years, this commingling was accompanied by a definite rise in overall quality, perhaps at the expense of the emergence of individual excellence which, paradoxically, in recent times has been far more rare in a landscape of illustrators who are much more determined in how they approach their work. The Illustrators Exhibition is a space where these changes become visible and obvious, and this is what makes it a place for valuable and essential debates around publishing.

It is certainty true that the exhibition represents a tremendous opportunity for illustrators, who find themselves with a wonderful showcase for their work, and the same applies to publishers: it is they who will choose, use and work with what they see on display. It would be very interesting to see how these opportunities have affected a certain kind of publishing and it would be just as interesting to take stock of the number of books that have come about because of the Exhibition. At the same time, the list of authors chosen at Bologna for their early work who then went on to become essential names in international illustration would be very long. Next year's milestone will be a good opportunity to stop, look back and try to determine this impressive historical baggage.

ROGER MELLO. NAU CATARINETA (MANATI PUBLISHING HOUSE)

13

Nowadays, thanks to magazines and the internet, illustrators have reached unprecedented levels of popularity in a trade that has not always been properly recognized. The number of illustrators who want to take part has expanded, and the Exhibition has managed to stay ahead of the transformations, adapting to this ever-changing reality. It has done so by cultivating relationships with some of the best international schools, which have long served as a link between the creators and the Fair itself. The involvement of many young illustrators and students has ensured that the Exhibition features a continuous renewal of ideas, styles and influences.

The quality of the choices that the Exhibition has managed to maintain in the face of the growing number of participants is also important thanks to the tremendous amount of care taken in selecting the jury: prominent illustrators, alert publishers, experts and professionals recognized in the worlds of publishing and illustration have maintained the elevated levels of quality, allowing the Illustrators Exhibition to continue building its future on top of its exceptional history.

The Illustrators Exhibition does not end with the Fair, however. Thanks to collaborative efforts with JBBY, the Japanese Board on Books for Young People, and the dedicated work of the Itabashi Art Museum (Tokyo), which has hosted the Exhibition and taken care of the international tour every year since 1978, the Exhibition will journey around Japan and other countries, further expanding its borders and its audience. From the experience at the Chicago Art Institute in the early 2000s to the recent delightful stop in Taiwan, as one of the main initiatives of the Taipei International Book Exhibition, after the grand tour of a number of different Japanese art museums, the Illustrators Exhibition continuously opens itself up to new experiences and its echo as a place of infinite possibilities for development. This is a precious legacy that can be shared with the public and become an outstanding educational opportunity about illustration for adults and children alike. The Japanese museums that host the Exhibition make it a central theme of their visits and workshops aimed at younger visitors, and this year Bologna will take up their example by offering a preview to families during the weekend preceding the Fair.

THE ILLUSTRATORS EXHIBITION IN JAPAN:

ITABASHI ART MUSEUM
ITABASHI (TOKYO)
4 JULY - 16 AUGUST 2015
WWW.ITABASHIARTMUSEUM.JP

OTANI MEMORIAL ART MUSEUM
NISHINOMIYA CITY
NISHINOMIYA (HYOGO)
22 AUGUST - 27 SEPTEMBER 2015
OTANIMUSEUM.JP/HOME

KAWARA MUSEUM
TAKAHAMA (AICHI)
3 OCTOBER - 1 NOVEMBER 2015
WWW.TAKAHAMA-KAWARA-MUSEUM.COM

ISHIKAWA NANAO ART MUSEUM
NANAO (ISHIKAWA)
6 NOVEMBER - 13 DICEMBER 2015
WWW.CITY.NANAO.ISHIKAWA.JP/NANABI

ROGER MELLO. NAU CATARINETA (MANATI PUBLISHING HOUSE)

ILLUSTRATORS EXHIBITION
JURY REPORT

PAOLA PARAZZOLI

ULLA RHEDIN

SVJETLAN JUNAKOVIĆ

CHARLES KIM

BENJAMIN CHAUD

Benjamin Chaud

Each year, the Bologna Children's Book Fair, the largest fair in the world for children's books, hosts a highly competitive Illustrators Exhibition. This year, almost 3000 professional and amateur illustrators from sixty-two countries sent in their art for consideration. A five-person jury selected seventy-six artists to include in the Exhibition, the main event of the fair. This year's jury members were Ulla Rhedin, a Swedish academic and specialist of picture books; widely published illustrators Svjetlan Junaković, from Croatia, and Benjamin Chaud, from France; Paola Parazzoli, an editor at Rizzoli Children's in Milan; and Charles Kim, associate publisher at The Museum of Modern Art, New York.

On January 11, we arrived in Bologna for a three-and-a-half-day marathon of seeing, debating, and selecting illustrators from all over the world. Bologna's culinary strengths and traditions are well known throughout Italy, and on the first night, our hosts – Illustrators Exhibition staff members Elena Pasoli, Roberta Chinni, Beatrice Monetti, and Runa Bignami – took us to a terrific local restaurant. The food and wine were superb, and we stayed out late, getting to know each other and discussing our criteria for selecting the artists.

Ushered the next morning at 9 into Hall 18 of the Bologna Fiere, we entered a massive, open space filled with long tables lined end to end. On them sat paintings and drawings of every kind and in all media, laid out in one large room. Thousands of submissions sat in tidy piles, each hoping to stand out, to impress a judge, to be selected for the big show.

It is daunting indeed to set eyes upon 15,000 original works on paper at once, and at least one juror panicked slightly. But the exhibition managers, well versed in the art of dividing and conquering, had sorted the works into very helpful categories, such as the country of the submitting artist, or whether the artist was previously published or unpublished. Submissions made by art schools and publishers on behalf of their artists occupied separate areas on one side of the room.

Being one of the less than 2.5% of entries chosen for the exhibition is not only an honour, it can change the illustrator's life forever. Over the course of four days, 25,000 people – publishers and editors, agents, authors, illustrators, students, and other professionals – roam the exhibition galleries, which sit in the middle of the enormous yet intimate fair. Dozens of illustrators, some of whom come out of complete obscurity, leave the exhibition with book contracts (both Junaković and Chaud have been selected multiple times for the exhibition).

Ulla Rhedin is a literary scholar, critic and lecturer, and a former jury member of the Astrid Lindgren Memorial Award, the "Nobel Prize" of children's books. She was looking for artists who could tell a story and push the boundaries of visual storytelling in picture books, and was especially interested in stories told from "the perspective of the child" in both text and pictures (this is seen as an aesthetic challenge to the authors/artists in Sweden). Chaud and Junaković, both of whom possess extensive knowledge of the styles and methods of their fellow illustrators, sought originality, proper composition, and a deft, original hand. As an editor in charge of producing over a dozen books a year for a prestigious Italian imprint, Parazzoli was on the lookout for talented artists to introduce to a large audience. Kim was simply looking for art that moved him, to be wowed by masterful lines and gorgeous colours. We all hoped to find artists who could convey emotion and humour to children, and express ideas clearly and inventively in ways we had rarely seen before.

We jurors spent some time on our own at the beginning, winding our way among the tables, absorbing the onslaught of colour, form, and line. Then, as a group, we selected artists who would make it into the second round, from which the final exhibition artists would be chosen. The jury made it through about 1,300 entries on the first day. We reached consensus quickly on most of the works, with occasional debates on the merits or weaknesses of an individual entrant.

We looked at all five works submitted by every single illustrator. Each juror's opinion held equal weight.

As the jury members began to go through each submission, pile by pile, table by table, a dazzling menagerie of animals and fantastical creatures jumped off the pages. Children and adults of all ages laughed, sang, cried, played, and slept in landscapes and buildings and interiors from all over the world. There were monsters and emperors and penguins, and several hundred bears, no two of them looking exactly alike. There were an unseemly number of cats, dogs, and owls, none of which remotely resembled each other either. We had all expected to see a wildly diverse group of illustrations, but none of us were prepared for the sheer individuality and uniqueness of the art.

But the coin had a flip side. The competition is open to anyone around the world who wants to apply, and many contestants were not fully aware of the limits of their talents. But the most common fault we could see was the lack of originality. Hundreds of very skilled artists were rejected because their work seemed too derivative to us. There were many excellent copies of Jean-Jacques Sempé, Saul Steinberg, Hayao Miyazaki, Maurice Sendak, Kitty Crowther – but they were copies nevertheless, treading on well-traveled ground.

Very few of the artists received a unanimous vote; most received no votes. Many only received one, but in several of those instances, the lone juror was able to convince the four others of the quality he or she saw. Many of the artists who made it into the final exhibition selection did so because a single juror fought for their work in the first round, while others had four votes on their side, only to have one juror argue persuasively against their inclusion in the show. At the end of that first day, after another lovely dinner filled with incredible food and genuine camaraderie, we did not make it back to the hotel until after 11:30. As we walked back from the restaurant, we looked up to see a sky filled with stars. Bologna is a modest and pretty city, and it has a special charm at night. On the second day, we paused from our task to speak for nearly an hour with a group of about twenty-five graduate students in illustration from Milan. We were told that a couple of them had submitted their work for consideration; we never found out who. Even with the break, we managed to judge over 1,700 entries on day two. Again, we looked at all five works from each contestant. Looking back, we are not certain how we were able to do this, but after two days, we had whittled the 3,000 artists to 166 finalists.

At times, we spent nearly an hour discussing whether an artist deserved to move forward, and why. One instance stands out as an example: Shuai Yue, a Chinese artist, had submitted five scenes or characters from the legendary Peking opera *Farewell My Concubine*. Made with acrylic paint on canvas, the paintings featured vibrant depictions of Xiang Yu, the famed King of Western Chu (232-202 BC) at the center of the opera, or soldiers in the heat of battle. In the background, ancient ideograms ran vertically down the canvas, whispering to us a centuries-old tale of love, sacrifice, honour, and death. One juror, Charles Kim, found the drawings breathtaking, but his fellow jurors did not. The artist had not sufficiently conveyed, in their opinion, a coherent storyline. They wondered how a publisher would reproduce these works in a book, and what could be done about the lines and lines of gray calligraphy. In the end, they felt the works were paintings, meant for a gallery or museum, but not illustrations, meant to accompany text in a children's book. But Kim was convinced that this work was an example of why we were there — to see new methods and mediums in storytelling, to step out of our comfort zones, and to allow illustrators to take risks to advance their craft. In the end, to Kim's great relief, the other jurors let the artist stay in the running.

At the start of day three, the jury members intentionally slowed down the process of reviewing the portfolios remaining. We were tired, and the hardest work lay ahead of us. Until then we had moved largely as a group, moving from table to table and coming to consensus on the artists to choose for the final round. Now we reviewed each of the 166 artists on our own, voting for our favourites using colour-coded stickers. When we were done, we gathered again to look at each finalist one by one. The artists who had received four or five votes were automatically selected for the exhibition; but only two dozen of them had earned that distinction. We debated at length the fate of the 140 or so others. Ultimately, the winning entrants showed a combination of freshness, a distinctive voice or point of view, and, most important, the ability to tell a compelling story using just five images. Technique often took a back seat to inventiveness; a perfectly realistic face or building was no match for a quirky, original world, hatched in a creative mind.

The Illustrators Exhibition managers never once told us what to do or what to select. Since they are Italians who manage an exhibition competition in Italy, it stands to reason that they might suggest that we choose more of their countrymen. They could have asked us to favor best-selling or well-known illustrators, or those coming from the largest markets, to help them market and publicize the exhibition. Instead, they stayed incredibly impartial and professional from start to finish, giving us help when we needed and avoiding any whiff of impropriety. Having asked us to be the jurors, they left us alone to do what they had asked us to do: select the artists. And that is what we did: we chose 76 "winners", who come from 22 countries on four continents. Several of them are widely published; many more have just started their careers or never been published. The veteran illustrators selected have proven that they still got it, while the newer talents are proof that the field of children's books is a dynamic one, with a steady supply of artists dreaming of a chance to introduce children to a world that resides, for now at least, in their imagination. And we, the jurors, left Bologna filled with enthusiasm for the books and artists that will fascinate and entertain our children, today and tomorrow.

Born in 1975 in the South of France, BENJAMIN CHAUD studied in Paris for 3 years at the École supérieure des arts appliqués, before moving to Strasbourg's École supérieure des arts décoratifs where he also studied for 3 years, after which he became illustrator. At the beginning of his career, he was twice selected for the Bologna Children's Book Fair. Benjamin has lived in both Marseille and Paris and now lives in the South of France. He is currently working with Hélium and Albin Michel in France and Chronicle Books in America. As well as illustrating stories by other writers, Benjamin also authors his own picturebooks.

Painter, illustrator and sculptor SVJETLAN JUNAKOVIĆ was born in 1961 in Zagreb, where he still lives. He graduated from Milan's Accademia di Belle Arti di Brera in 1985 and has had personal shows in numerous cities including Munich, Brussels, Monza, Budapest, Siena, Ljubljana, Zagreb, Naples, Genoa and Mexico City. Over the years Svjetlan focused increasingly on writing and illustrating children's books, working with a range of publishers in more than twenty countries including the United States, Japan, South Korea, Italy, Austria, Germany, Switzerland, Mexico, Argentina, Chile, Spain, Portugal, the Netherlands and Finland. His work has been exhibited at major children's illustration venues, receiving numerous awards: the IBBY Certificate of Honour in New Delhi in 1998; the 2001 Bratislava Biennial of Illustration (BIB); the 2003 Award of the city of Bari for the best foreign illustrator published in Italy; the 2004 award at Japan's OITA Biennial; and the Zagreb Awards in 1994, 1998, 1999, 2003 and 2004. Svjetlan also won the 2002 Zagreb Biennial of Illustration prize. He was selected for the Illustrators Exhibition at the Bologna Children's Book Fair in 1995, 1997, 1998, 1999, 2002, 2004 and 2005. In 2006 he received the Grand Prix at the Zagreb International Biennial of Illustration, and in 2007 the Spanish Culture Ministry's prize for the best edited infant and juvenile book. 2008 saw him win a Special Mention in the Bologna Ragazzi Award Fiction section and the H.C. Andersen award at the Sestri Levante festival for the best illustrated book in Italy. Svjetlan authored the cartoon *My Way*, which received several prizes around the world. He has also written scripts for films and puppet shows staged in theatres in Slovenia, Lubljana and Maribor. Currently Svjetlan teaches illustration at the International Summer School in Sarmede, Italy, and is a faculty member of the Zagreb Academy of Fine Arts. He holds courses on illustration and speaks at a range of training events in several Italian cities (Rome, Treviso, Padua, Monza, Verona etc.). He was also Croatia's candidate for the 2008 and 2010 IBBY-HCA Awards and is acknowledged as one of the five best illustrators in the world.

CHUL R. (CHARLES) KIM is Associate Publisher at The Museum of Modern Art, New York (MoMA), where he oversees the digital-publishing strategy, intellectual property and copyright issues, and international collaborations for both print and digital projects. He also supervises a line of children's books and serves on the MoMA Kids Committee, which guides the Museum's retail and other strategies for younger audiences. He previously served for nine years as Director of Publications and Editor-in-Chief of the Cooper Hewitt, Smithsonian Design Museum in New York. He earned his MA in French Literature at New York University and was a Fulbright Scholar in France.

PAOLA PARAZZOLI was born and lives in Milan. Even as a young child she showed a consuming interest in books and pictures, a trait encouraged by her family and which led her to graduate in Letters with a final History of Art dissertation on illustrations in Italian books at the turn of the 19th century. While at university Paola started working as an editor at AMZ, a children's book publisher. She then moved to De Agostini, and finally to Rizzoli ragazzi where for many years she has worked on children's picture book projects. Two important landmarks in her career were the writing and art direction of the fairy story and illustrated Bible story collections that came out in 2005 and 2008 with the Italian dailies "Corriere della Sera" and "Il Sole 24 Ore". In the last ten years Paola has worked with the design school Istituto Europeo di Design (IED) in Milan and Turin, and since 2008 has taught at the Masters course Illustrating for Publishing, part of the Macerata Ars in Fabula training project. She has held workshops at Milan's Mimaster of Illustration and courses on picture books for primary school children. Paola has also been a part of Italian venues like Isola delle storie in Gavoi and Tuttestorie in Sardinia, and the Festivaletteratura in Mantua. A great admirer of illustrators, Paola has promised herself that one day she would like to become an apprentice illustrator.

ULLA RHEDIN is a Swedish literary scholar, critic and writer of theoretical works and articles on picturebook theory. Born in Falköping, Sweden on 9 January 1946, Ulla has taught drama, film and children's books at various universities since 1969, particularly at Karlstad University (1972-2000). In 1993, Ulla received a PhD in Comparative Literature from the University of Gothenburg. Since then she has taught picturebook theory as associate professor and senior lecturer, first in Karlstad and currently at the University Colleges of Arts, Crafts and Design in Stockholm and Gothenburg. Her thesis, *Bilderboken – på väg mot en teori*, Alfabeta 1992, 2001 ("The picturebook – towards a theory"), she argues that as a medium and art form in its own right, the picturebook should be considered in a new theoretical frame based on multi-media, visual and literary concepts. Since 1980 Ulla has been a critic with the Swedish daily, "Dagens Nyheter", Stockholm, where her articles and picturebook reviews focus on the performative, multi-media and interdisciplinary aspects of the picturebook. One of Ulla's main concepts is the aesthetic-psychological challenge posed for (single or dual) picturebook narrators in adopting the child's perspective. Between 2002-2014, Ulla was a member of the first ALMA (the Astrid Lindgren Memorial Award) jury. Ulla lives on the island of Tjörn where she has been involved in several projects concerning picturebooks and seminars for illustrators in cooperation with The Nordic Watercolour Museum in Skärhamn, Tjörn. In this context she was one of the editors of a Nordic poetics of picturebooks, *En fanfar för bilderboken* (Alfabeta 2013, "A fanfare for the picturebook") with contributions from Gro Dahle (Norway), Oscar K (Denmark), Maria Laukka (Finland), Gunna Grähs and Ulla Rhedin (Sweden).

2015 BOLOGNA ILLUSTRATORS EXHIBITION

PUBLISHER'S NOTE:

AS STATED IN THE EXHIBITION REGULATIONS,

EACH ILLUSTRATOR SUBMITTED TO THE JURY

A SEQUENCE OF FIVE IMAGES, WHICH IDEALLY

FORM A STORY. IN SOME CASES, WE DECIDED

TO REPRODUCE ONLY SOME OF THE ILLUS-

TRATIONS SO AS TO HIGHLIGHT THE STRENGTHS

THAT THE JURY SAW IN THE WORK OF EACH

ARTIST. BUT WE ALSO DECIDED TO MAIN-

TAIN THE ORIGINAL NUMBERS IN THE CAPTIONS

OF THE ILLUSTRATIONS THAT WERE PRESENTED,

WHERE NOT EXPLICITLY STATED OTHERWISE,

ILLUSTRATORS HAVE NOT BEEN PREVIOUSLY

PUBLISHED ELSEWHERE.

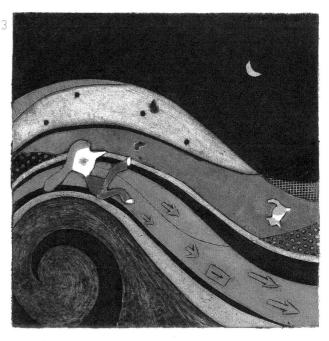

2

3

4

5

1-2 WALKING AT NIGHT   3 WINDY NIGHT   4 RAINY NIGHT   5 SHARING THE NIGHT TOGETHER

KYOUNGMI AHN

KYOUNGMIAHN.COM

The nights • Collagraph • Fiction

Republic of Korea • *Busan, 4 April 1975*

km_ahn@hotmail.com • 0082 10 44834429

1

ACCADEMIA DI BELLE ARTI DI BOLOGNA
DIRECTOR: ENRICO FORNAROLI
COORDINATOR: EMILIO VARRÀ

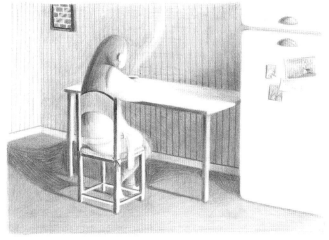

1 THERE WAS A PLACE THAT SHE KNEW WELL 2 EVEN IF SHE HAD NEVER REALLY SEEN IT 3 EVERY DAY SHE STOPPED AND THOUGHT ABOUT HOW SHE COULD GET THERE 4 SO SHE WENT OUT IN THE MORNING 5 AND STARTED LOOKING FOR IT. WATCHING THE SKY

ELIANA ALBERTINI
ELIANALBERTINI.TUMBLR.COM

Ricerca (Search) · Coloured pencils · Fiction

Italy · *Adria, 13 February 1992*

eliana.albertini@gmail.com · 0039 3470744212

"POLVO DE ROCA". A BUEN PASO. BARCELONA. 2014
"LE GÉANT DES MARAIS". OQO EDITORA. PONTEVEDRA. 2013
"LE MORCEAUX D'AMOUR". AUTREMENT JEUNESSE. PARIS. 2012
"VEUX-TU DEVENIR BÊTE". HONGFEI CULTURES. AMBOISE. 2012

2

3

4

5

GÉRALDINE ALIBEU

GERALDINEALIBEU.COM

Paysages et créatures (Landscapes and creatures)

Collage, marker, pencil • Fiction

France • *Echirolles, 16 February 1978*

alibeugeraldine@gmail.com • 0033 6 22205536

DAVID DANIEL ÁLVAREZ HERNÁNDEZ

ESCAMASDEPLATA.BLOGSPOT.COM · DAVID-ALVAREZ.BLOGSPOT.MX

The ancient night · Oil and acrylic paint · Fiction

Mexico · *Mexico D.F., 3 August 1984*

alvarezhdavid@gmail.com · 0052 65979701

1

5

3

SANGSUN AN
INSTAGRAM.COM/ANSANGSUN

Ego • Silk screen and stencil • Fiction

Republic of Korea • *Suwon City, 11 October 1979*

hungrytoo99@naver.com • **0082 1027633760**

1 I DON'T HAVE ANY TIGERS AND RABBITS   2 I AM SMALL   3 I AM FEARFUL AT TIMES   5 THANKS TO YOU. I'M VERY PLEASED

3

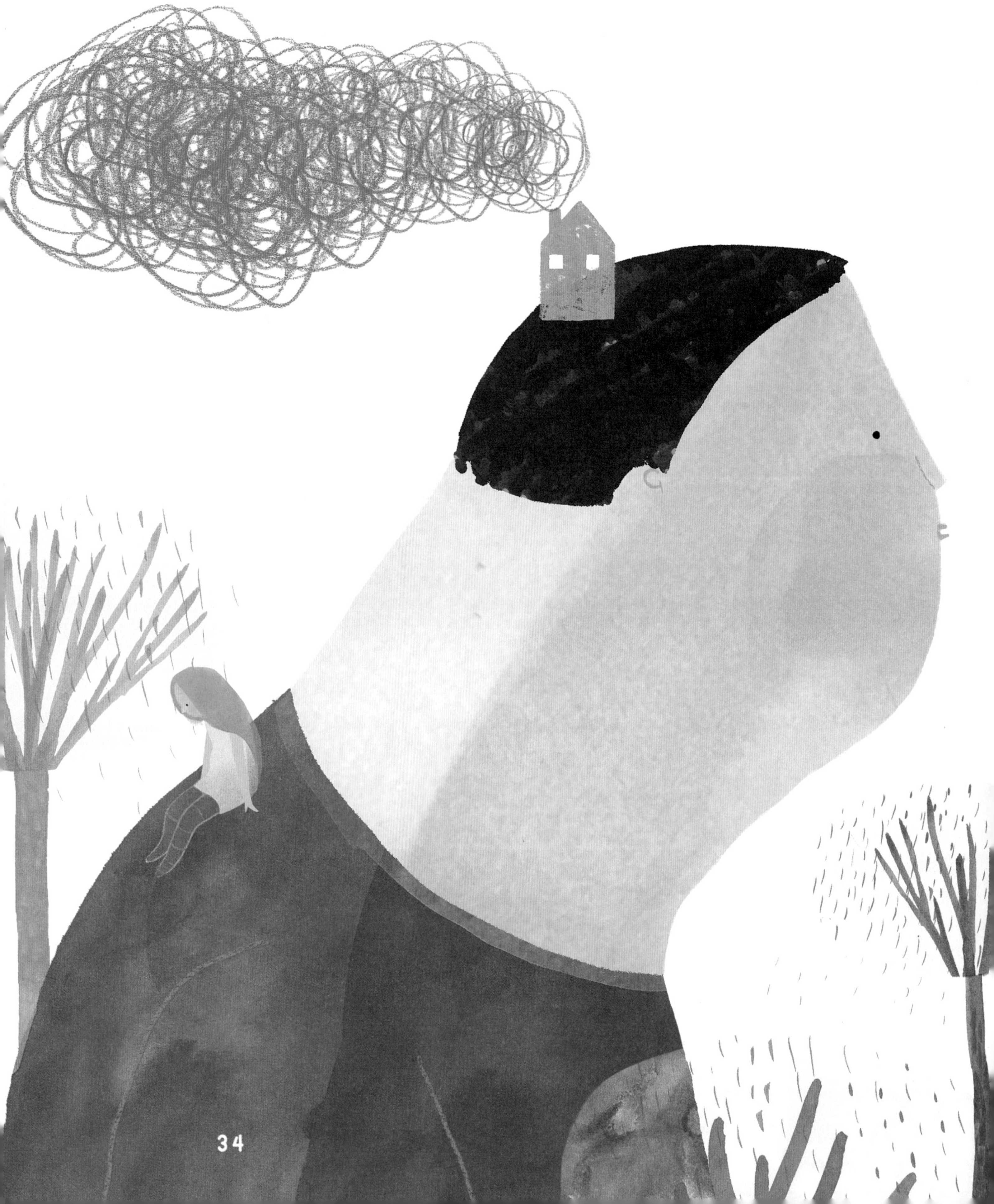

2

4

5

GLADYS BACCALA

GLADILLA.TUMBLR.COM

Dreaming of Giants and Little Beings · Mixed media · Fiction

Switzerland · *Locarno, 23 July 1981*

gladys.art@gmail.com · 0041 079 3646720

"RAAF REE, LEES JE MEE?", GOTTMER, HAARLEM, 2011
"AAP BEER CHEETA", GOTTMER, HAARLEM, 2009

4

HENRIETTE BOERENDANS

BOERENDANS.COM

Nul is een raar getal (Zero is a strange number) • Woodcut • Non Fiction
Gottmer, Haarlem, 2013, ISBN 9789025753511
The Netherlands • *Delft, 16 January 1966*
henriette@boerendans.com • **0031 020 6160118**

1

2

"MR. WILDERS STAR", CARLSEN, HAMBURG, 2014
"THE POET FROM VANLOESE", CARLSEN, HAMBURG, 2013
"I'M LOOKING AND LOOKING AND LOOKING", CARLSEN, HAMBURG, 2012
"ONE SHOULD THINK CAREFULLY WHEN YOU WANT TO DRINK TEA WITH MRS. BIRD", CARLSEN, HAMBURG, 201
"THE LAND OF THE DOOMED PUPPIES", CARLSEN, HAMBURG, 2012
"THE UGLY CHILDREN", CARLSEN, HAMBURG, 2011
"MY BROTHER AND I GO OUT", GYLDENDAL, KØBENHAVN, 2011
"LITTLEBROTHER", GYLDENDAL, KØBENHAVN, 2010
"A CHRISTMAS STORY", CARLSEN, HAMBURG, 2010
"THE STORY ABOUT THE LITTLE SWEET PIGGY", GYLDENDAL, KØBENHAVN, 2009
"SNABELS HERBARIUM", CARLSEN, HAMBURG, 2007

RASMUS BREGNHOI

RASMUSBREGNHOI.DK • INSTAGRAM.COM/RASMUSBREGNHOI

The Story of Ib Madsen • Digital media • Fiction

Høst and Søn, Copenhagen, 2013, ISBN 9878763827430

Denmark • *Asminderød, 4 June 1965*

rasmus@rasmusbregnhoi.dk • 0045 26164635

"SIN ZAPATOS NO ME ATO". EDITORIAL CARÀ CATÀ. BUENOS AIRES. 2012

5 THE HOUSE IN THE WOODS   4 TRAVEL TO THE COUNTRY   3 THE ESCAPE   2 THE BETRAYAL   1 THE RUSE

MARÍA FLORENCIA CAPELLA

FLORENCIACAPELLA.COM.AR

El Convite (The banquet) • Digital media • Fiction

Argentina • *Buenos Aires, 30 October 1981*

info@florenciacapella.com.ar • 0054 911 67934929

ÉCOLE ESTIENNE (ESAIG)
SCHOOL DIRECTOR: ARMELLE NOUIS
COORDINATOR: STÉPHANE SOULARUE

42

LAURINE
CHARPENTIER
LILIELESTRAT.TUMBLR.COM

Layers • Gouache, acrylics and
coloured pencils • Non Fiction

France

La Garenne Colombes, 19 May 1994

pepin.dabricot@outlook.fr

0033 0621391980

1

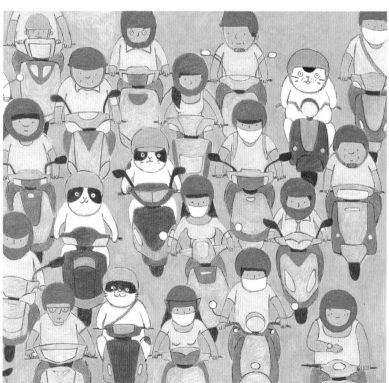

2

3

4

1 WHEN I WAS A KID, I ENJOYED RIDING THE BICYCLE WITH MY DAD   2 NOW AS A PARENT, I RIDE A MOTORCYCLE. TRAVELLING BACK AND FORTH IN THE TRAFFIC AND FIGHTING FOR MY BELOVED FAMILY   3 THE GOODS I DELIVER ARE FILLED WITH PEOPLE'S DREAMS WHICH SUPPORT THEIR BELIEFS   4 THE MOST PLEASANT MOMENT IS THE RIDE WITH MY WIFE AND KID AFTER WORK, HANGING AROUND THE PORT IN WHICH I WORK   5 SOMEDAY I'LL TELL MY KID ABOUT MY CHILDHOOD MEMORIES OF TAKING A RIDE IN THE FIELD WITH HIS GRANDPARENTS. BUT NOW, IT'S MY TURN TO TAKE HIM AROUND, TO ANY PLACE HE WANTS

YU LIN CHEN
FACEBOOK.COM/BRAMASOLO2

The ride to happiness • Coloured pencils, acrylic • Fiction

Taiwan • *Taipei, 5 July 1981*

bramasoloster@gmail.com • 00886 916752700

"A BOY AND A JAGUAR". HOUGHTON MIFFLIN HARCOURT. BOSTON. 2014
"THE LONGEST NIGHT". SCHWARTZ & WADE. NEW YORK. 2013
"MY BLUE IS HAPPY". CANDLEWICK PRESS. SOMMERVILLE. 2013
"SEA SERPENT AND ME". HOUGHTON MIFFLIN HARCOURT. BOSTON. 2008

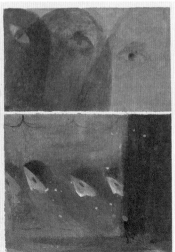

1 COVER   2 MIDNIGHT TRAIN RIDE   3 MEETING A FRIEND IN THE TRAIN STATION AND WALKING ON A TIGHT ROPE
4 TIGHT ROPE LEADING INTO A FLOATING HOUSE ABOVE A LAKE   5 HOUSE WITH WHISPERING WALLS AND GHOSTS

CATIA CHIEN
CATIACHIEN.COM · FACEBOOK.COM/CATIA-CHIEN

Maps · Acrylic · Fiction

USA · *São Paulo, Brazil, 25 August 1978*

catiachien@gmail.com · **001 6268333696**

"DUE ALI". TOPIPITTORI. MILAN. TO BE PUBLISHED
"IL PICCOLO CESARE". EDITORI LATERZA. ROME. 2014
"FAVOLE PER BAMBINI SPIRITOSI". "FAVOLE PER BAMBINI NOTTAMBULI". "FAVOLE
PER BAMBINI CURIOSI". "FAVOLE PER BAMBINI POETI". "FAVOLE PER BAMBINI GOLOSI"
IN "ENCICLOPEDIA DELLA FAVOLA". EDITORI INTERNAZIONALI RIUNITI. ROME. 2002
"I TRE PORCELLINI". DE AGOSTINI. MILAN. 1999

1

3

4

5

1 ERNEST   2 RITA   3 SAM   4 PAOLINO – HOMAGE TO BRUNO ANGOLETTA   5 PHIL

MARIACHIARA DI GIORGIO
MARIACHIARADIGIORGIO.BLOGSPOT.COM

Five characters · Mixed media · Fiction

Italy · *Rome, 27 April 1983*

mariachiaradigiorgio@gmail.com · **0039 331 4161718**

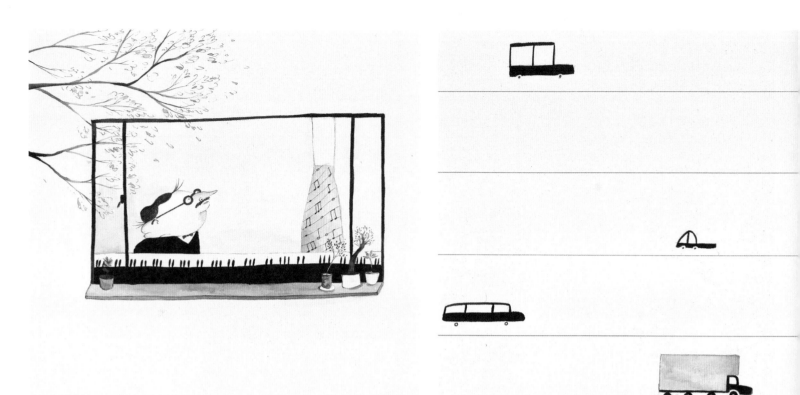

2

3

4

5

"GREEN FRIDAYS". RANDOM HOUSE — LUMEN. COLOMBIA. 2015
"CAT BOY". SM. COLOMBIA. 2013
"THE ELEPHANT'S TRIP". ED GATO MALO. COLOMBIA. 2011
"TWO LITTLE BIRDS". RANDOM HOUSE — LUMEN. COLOMBIA. 2011
"JACINTO AND MARIA JOSÉ". FCE. 2009
"THEY ARE ALL JOKING". NORMA. COLOMBIA. 2007
"THE MOST FEROCIOUS ANIMAL". NORMA. COLOMBIA. 2007

El bajo Alberti (Alberti bass) • Inks • Fiction
Penguin Random House, 2014, ISBN 9789588639499
Colombia • *Bogotà, 25 April 1984*
dipacho.com@gmail.com • 0057 5284038

DIPACHO
DIPACHO.COM
FACEBOOK.COM/DIPACHOILUSTRADOR
DIPACHO.BLOGSPOT.COM

1-5 ALBERTI BASS

1

2

3

CAMBRIDGE SCHOOL OF ART
SCHOOL DIRECTOR: CHRIS OWEN
COORDINATOR: MARTIN SALISBURY

4

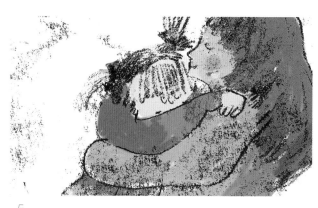

5

JENNY DUKE

JENNYDUKE.CO.UK

Where did you go today? · Monoprint and digital print · Fiction

Great Britain · *Manchester, 22 July 1954*

jenny@jennyduke.co.uk · 0044 7702342422

1

Not sure why I don't fit in ?

2

I love it mum!

3

Don't worry I will help you!

"MY FIRST ORCHESTRA BOOK". NAXOS BOOKS. HONG KONG. 2014
"RELATEDNESS IN ASSISTED REPRODUCTION". CAMBRIDGE UNIVERSITY PRESS. CAMBRIDGE. 2014
"LITTLE BIG BOOKS" - ILLUSTRATIONS FOR CHILDREN'S PICTURE BOOKS (BOOKCOVER).
GESTALTEN. BERLIN. 2012

what are you wearing?

Don't think you will bother me now.....

You have to keep it a secret...

1 NOT SURE WHY I DON'T FIT IN   2 WHAT ARE YOU WEARING?   3 DON'T WORRY. I WILL HELP YOU!   4 YOU HAVE TO KEEP IT A SECRET   5 DON'T THINK YOU WILL BOTHER ME NOW

KARIN EKLUND

KARINEKLUND.COM • FACEBOOK.COM/KARIN.EKLUND

Fitting in • Pencil, marker pen, pen on paper • Fiction

Sweden • *Lund, 10 September 1974*

keklund@hotmail.com • 0044 1223359638

5

MARIA GABRIELLA GASPARRI

GABRIELLAGASPARRI.BLOGSPOT.IT

"Great Expectations" – Charles Dickens • Pencil, crayon, ecoline, linocut on paper • Fiction

Italy • *Naples, 6 April 1976*

gabriella.gasp@gmail.com • 0039 331 2048026

1 PIP HIDES HIS BREAD AND BUTTER, TO TAKE TO MAGWITCH   5 PIP, HERBERT, STARTOP HELPS MAGWITCH ESCAPE

3

2

5

4

FATEMEH GHASEMI
BEHANCE.NET/FATEMEHGHASEMI

My beautiful mom • Oil colour, acrylic • Fiction

Iran • *Ghom, 17 April 1979*

maryam33@gmail.com • 0098 2177626946

"LA STORIA DI NABUCCO", EUM EDIZIONI UNIVERSITÀ DI MACERATA, 2013

FRANCESCO GIUSTOZZI

FRANCESCOGIUSTOZZI.BLOGSPOT.IT · BEHANCE.NET/FRANCESCOGIUSTOZZI

Le lieu du crime (The place of the crime) · Digital media · Non fiction

Éditions Milan, Paris, to be published

Italy · *Macerata, 18 May 1986*

francesco.giustozzi@hotmail.it · 0039 333 1385337

"1913". AED STUDIO BEOGRAD. BELGRAD. 2014

HAW HAMBURG
SCHOOL DIRECTOR. DOROTHEA WENZEL
COORDINATOR. CHRISTIAN HAHN

2

3

4

5

BENJAMIN GOTTWALD

BENJAMINGOTTWALD.TUMBLR.COM

BACHWALD.TUMBLR.COM

Blickfeld (Visual field) • Mixed media • Fiction

Germany • *Darmstadt, 17 May 1987*

benjamin.gottwald@web.de • 0049 015 78 1987388

1 A BIG LOCOMOTIVE HAS PULLED INTO TOWN./HEAVY, HUMUNGUS, WITH SWEAT ROLLING DOWN./A PLUMP JAMBO OLIVE./HUFFING AND PUFFING AND PANTING AND SMELLY./FIRE BELCHES FORTH FROM HER FAT CAST IRON BELLY.   2 NUMEROUS WAGONS SHE TUGS DOWN THE TRACK:/IRON AND STEEL MONSTERS HITCHED UP TO HER BACK.   3 ALL FILLED WITH PEOPLE AND OTHER THINGS TOO:/THE FIRST CARRIES CATTLE, THEN HORSES NOT FEW:/THE THIRD CAR WITH CORPULENT PEOPLE IS FILLED./EATING FAT FRANKFURTERS ALL FRESHLY GRILLED./THE FOURTH CAR

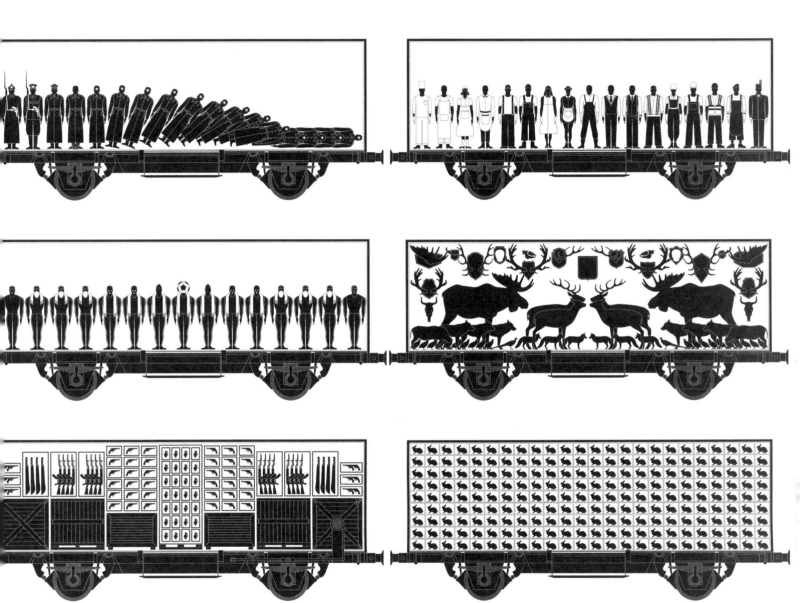

IS PACKED TO THE HILT WITH BANANAS./THE FIFTH HAS A CARGO OF SIX GRAND PI-AN-AS.   4 THE SIXTH WAGON CARRIES A CANNON OF STEEL./WITH HEAVY IRON GIRDERS BENEATHE EVERY WHEEL./THE SEVENTH HAS TABLES. OAK CUPBOARDS WITH PLATES./WHILE AN ELEPHANT. BEAR. TWO GIRAFFES FILL THE EIGHTH./THE NINTH CONTAINS NOTHING BUT WELL-FATTENED SWINE./IN THE TENTH: BAGS AND BOXES. NOW ISN'T THAT FINE?   5 THERE MUST BE AT LEAST FORTY CARS IN A ROW./AND WHAT THEY ALL CARRY/I SIMPLY DON'T KNOW...

MALGORZATA GUROWSKA

FACEBOOK.COM/MALGORZATA.GUROWSKA

The locomotive/IDEOLO • Digital media, offset • Non Fiction

Artificial Foundation, Warsaw, 2014, ISBN 9788364011047

Poland • *Warsaw, 6 June 1977*

m_box@tlen.pl • 0048 691031944

What is the importance, both from an illustrator's and from a publisher's point of view, of spaces such as the BCBF's Illustrators Exhibition?

First of all, I think the Exhibition represents an opportunity for both groups to find a trajectory towards which illustration is headed. The exhibition takes place every year, but each year reveals a different plan. Illustrations by established and younger artists interact with each other: the established ones offer languages and styles that can be inspirational to the emerging ones, in a panorama that is always presenting new ideas. Beyond the danger of plagiarism (which exists, and always has existed in art history, otherwise artistic currents would not develop), there is a fruitful exchange between senior and junior illustrators, the younger ones are enriched with the expressive code of the elders, they assimilate and exceed it with their freshness, always moving the limit further and further. This is why the Exhibition is an interesting place both for illustrators and for publishers. Illustrators can come face to face with the richness of the language presented, while publishers can find a panorama of artists who can be inspiring.

How can you recognise the narrative force of an illustration?

There are many elements that make an illustration a narrative. But when you are talking about picture books, the weight of the narration doesn't tend to fall on one single image: it is the sequence of images that tells the story. It does remain true that a single image can have an inherently narrative force. Think of cover images. The style and colours often seek to communicate something about the book's contents, sometimes even going beyond that, playing with the title. But when talking about picture books, we must speak about illustrations in the plural. In this case, it is in the transition from one illustration to the next, in the connection, where you discover the narrative rhythm. We look for the storytelling in the rhythm. The illustrations are like notes on the score: their position, the way in which they form a connection, the harmonies and the dissonances that we perceive between them to form the narrative images. The sequence of the layers, the details, the solids and the voids, the expression of the characters and the colours used are all elements that collectively make up a strong and communicative illustration. It is not given that illustration ought to follow what is said in the text. Indeed, often the power of icons is in knowing how to relate something beyond the text, in suggesting what is left unsaid.

The illustrator often manages to tell a complementary or parallel story through the images. Take the example of *Hänsel and Gretel*, illustrated by Lorenzo Mattotti. The book is extraordinarily evocative, it immediately places us in the protagonists' point of view, and manages to bring out of the children's anguish and fear of being lost in the woods through the deliberate choice of powerful blacks and whites. Here the reader is completely swept away by the story.

How can an editor help an author – or authors, if the project is a collaboration between an illustrator and a writer – to help improve an illustrated book?

Here you are really dealing with two separate cases. When there is a single author, this never really becomes an issue. The author-illustrator already has the story in mind, both in terms of the written text and the visual part. It is difficult for the editor to intervene in these cases. I can give you an example. When Alessandro Sanna brought *Fiume lento*, we didn't have any objections, there was no editorial intervention. We chose the graphic apparatus together (the format, art for the cover and the inside, the font, the type of paper), important things, but there was never any intervention on his story.

In the case of a book that has been produced jointly by a writer and an illustrator, the editor's work is different: they must be able to act with discretion. The editor must never try to replace the writer: don't rewrite, but suggest. They have to be able to help the writer find a way to channel his story, suggesting what to change in the text (round out a character, cut parts, deepen others).

The same applies to the illustrator. I ask illustrators to prepare a storyboard of the book, because it can give me an idea of the book's rhythm and the pace of the visual narrative. Younger illustrators often want to impress at all costs and they are likely to lean towards aestheticism, looking at special effects and losing sight of the functionality of the image. They love close-ups, for example, ignoring the fact that they are difficult to manage on the page and they can be disturbing. And this is where the editor intervenes: suggesting what size the images should be, the shots, the points of view and proposing that they delete what is unnecessary. I had an aesthetics professor at university who showed us how to distinguish between what is essential and functional within a composition and, on the contrary, what is superfluous. Each detail must make sense; sometimes removing things helps to strengthen an image's energy.

You were selected twice at the Bologna Children's Book Fair at the start of your career. What impact has that reward had on your career?

JUROR
**POINT
OF VIEW
BENJAMIN
CHAUD**

I was still a student when I was selected for the first time, I remember being thrilled. I went to the Bologna Children's Book Fair to show my work, and that was where I met my first publisher who then took on the project that I was presenting. I was selected again the following year and I presented some drawings that were later released by the same publisher. Being selected brought me a great deal of visibility, it allowed me to take my first steps in this career (which are always the most difficult) and, most of all, it gave me self-confidence. I had been accepted into this wonderful world of children's books.

The third time I was here, I presented illustrations from a book that had already been published and I wasn't selected. I decided that I would no longer participate in the contest to make room for younger artists, and also because I was afraid that I would no longer be selected.

It is because of this that I agreed with the jury when we decided to give priority to illustrators who have not yet been published, or have been published only recently.

Should a good illustrator have a recognisable style?

Of course. More than a style, an illustrator must have their own universe, a way of seeing and representing the world. Before it becomes a beautiful image, an illustration is the view that one person has on a story, and it must speak about something personal to be able to touch the readers.

They obviously don't come to us out of thin air and we all have our own influences, but we must try to have as many as we can and be stimulated by everything: painting, theatre, cinema... and not only in children's illustration. For me, having a style means knowing how to understand and accept your flaws so that they become part of your personal mode of expression. This isn't easy, it's much easier to find faults in others and we tend to try to hide our own, wanting to be someone else. I once had a teacher who told us: "go towards the things that others don't like in you. That is you."

Compared to non-illustrators, do illustrators have more tools at their disposal to be able to judge the work of other illustrators or is there a risk of looking at it through the filter of their own work?

There is certainly a risk, and the jury is aware of that. I can't remove my own filter, and I think that it allows me to effectively judge some aspects of the images that were presented to us: composition, lines, originality (although I am not infallible). I have been an illustrator for 16 years now and I think that, more than anything else, it is my ability to see that has grown. I am not more skilful or more inspired than I was at the beginning of my career, but I am better at being able to see outside of myself and see how others are faring.

For the less technical aspects of the images presented, I always try to put myself in the shoes of a child seeing them for the first time, and I think I do it well. A drawing can be completely off, yet still be funny, touching, sensitive, intelligent... and so it becomes a very good illustration. There are other members of the jury who come from other parts of the book world, each with their own gaze that we have had to overcome in order to reach a consensus on the images that we have selected.

Can you list three qualities that you think a children's illustrator absolutely must have?

First of all, an illustrator must be able to create a story through images. The difference between an illustration and other types of artistic images is precisely its narrative potential. The "tale" for images must have a certain pattern, so that the story becomes lively and dynamic. The rhythm is created by balancing the composition, with the use of colour, but also with the choices related to the book's plot.

SVJETLAN JUNAKOVIĆ. THE JURY

The second quality that an illustrator must have, which is no less important than the first, is a style that reflects their own feelings. The drawing must be recognisable, original and technically valid. That doesn't mean that the artist needs to become a mannerist and create all books in the same way. On the contrary, they should look for a style that is suitable for each book and a technique that helps to express its message in the best possible way. Illustrators must be open to contemporary art, a field where, just as in illustration, the expression of the concept, of the content, is becoming the most important part of the project.

I would propose a personal attribute as the third quality: children's illustration, in my opinion, ought to be witty. Speaking to children with amusing illustrations is, for me, the ultimate goal in communication between the illustrators and whoever is looking at or reading the book.

What is the identity of an illustrator?

You can recognise the identity through the freedom that the illustrators can allow themselves when creating the image, in designing the book. To achieve freedom, the illustrators must paint or draw images that are not necessarily linked to publishing. They must feel like artists, who create works according to their own feelings. Only after having experimented in a free and creative way can an illustrator develop a style that best represents the author's personality.

Books aren't bought directly by their target audience, but by adult guardians (parents, grandparents, aunts and uncles). Do you think this has some impact on the illustrator's work?

I don't think so. Many illustrators do not cater directly to their target audience when designing their books, it would be very limiting to only think about what could please a child. Each child is very different, it wouldn't be possible to create a book that all of them would like. One important aspect is to teach the adults (those who buy the books) to read them together with their children or grandchildren so as to accompany them in a critical reading, making them appreciate what is beautiful in the design, focusing on the artistic aspect. Flicking through a book with children in this way could be a nice start to a number of different conversations, of better relationships between young and old, and of a funnier, more beautiful life!

4

CAMBRIDGE SCHOOL OF ART
SCHOOL DIRECTOR: CHRIS OWEN
COORDINATOR: MARTIN SALISBURY

1

1 EMILY. ROSE. FATHER AND MRS. PERKINS ALL LIVED TOGETHER IN A BIG HOUSE IN THE COUNTRYSIDE

2 EMILY AND ROSE LIKED TO DO LOTS OF THINGS. BUT MOST OF ALL THEY LIKED TO LOOK IN THE GLASSHOUSE

4 INSIDE THE GLASSHOUSE WAS STILL AND QUIET. THERE WAS NO SIGN OF THE GHOST

2

KATIE HARNETT

KATIEHARNETT.COM · @KATIE_HARNETT

The Ghost in the Glasshouse · Gouache, pencil crayon, watercolour, digital media · Fiction

Great Britain · *Sheffield, 16 January 1989*

katieharnett@hotmail.com · 0044 07712161455

"KOMMT EIN BOOT", RESIDENZ VERLAG, GRAZ, 2012
"JAKOB & DAS ROTE BUCH", WIENER DOM-VERLAG, WIEN, 2012
"DER STERNENBLÄTTERBAUM", RESIDENZ VERLAG, GRAZ, 2011
"DR. CHICKENSOUP", RESIDENZ VERLAG, GRAZ, 2011
"OJE, SAGT DIE FEE", RESIDENZ VERLAG, GRAZ, 2010
"HASENLENZ", RESIDENZ VERLAG, GRAZ, 2010
"SCHLAF GUT, SUSI! SCHLAF GUT, SCHLAF!", RESIDENZ VERLAG, GRAZ, 2009

Der verliebte Koch (The enamoured cook)

Pencil, watercolour, acrylic • Fiction

Luftschachtverlag, Wien, 2015

Austria • *Vienna, 7 December 1969*

ask@gruenstich.at • 0043 69919531974

VERENA HOCHLEITNER

GRUENSTICH.AT

FACEBOOK.COM/FRIEDERIKE.GRUNSTICH

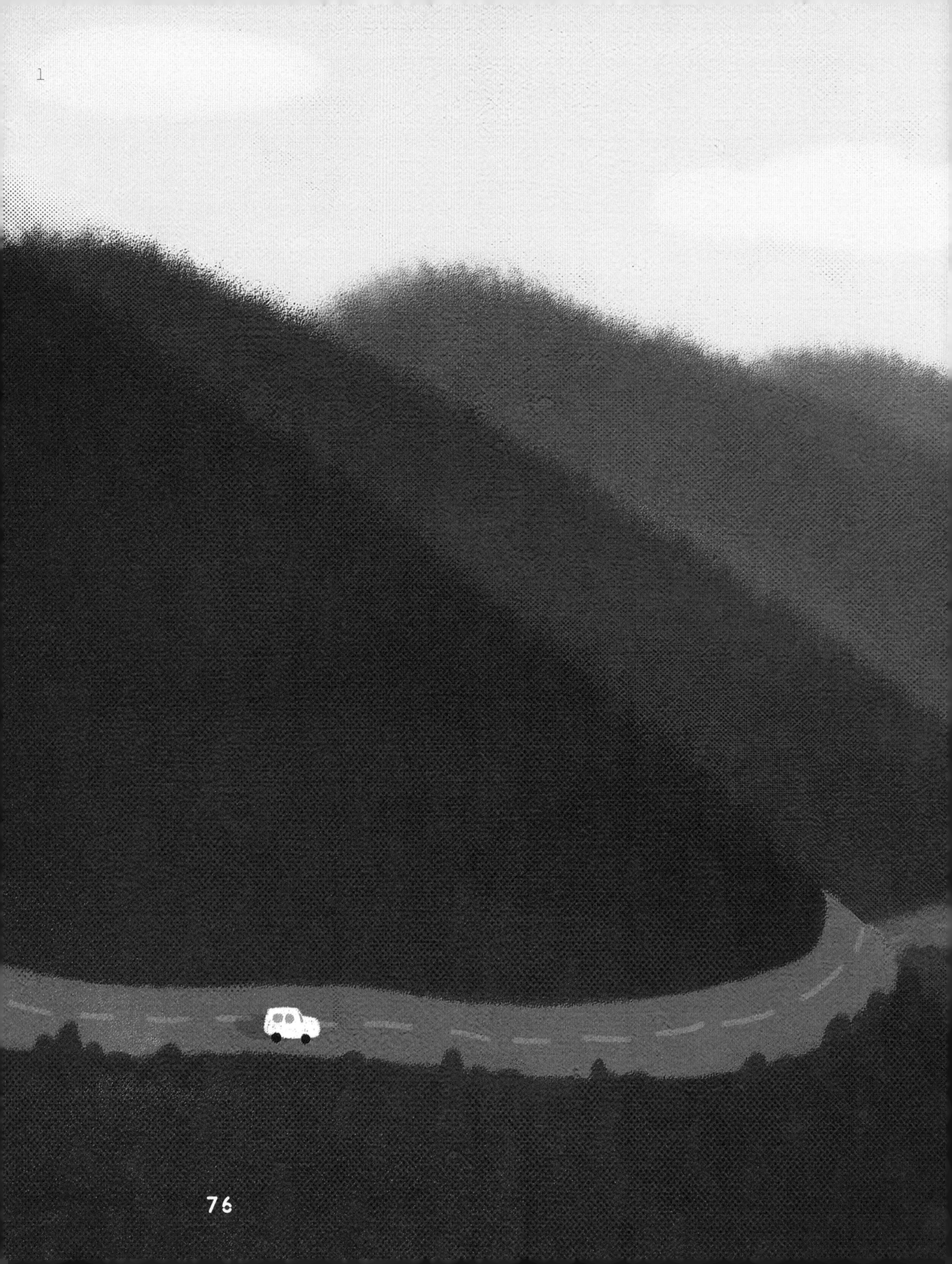

2

3

4

5

1 HELLO, WORLD! 2 DOWN AN UNKNOWN ROAD 3 WANDERING 4 I'LL BE THERE SOMEDAY 5 I CAN GO THE DISTANCE

LEILEI HUANG
LEILEIHUANG.COM · LEILEIHUANG.TUMBLR.COM

Go the Distance · Digital media · Fiction

China · *Sichuan, 30 January 1992*

leilei.huang@hotmail.com · 0044 07510792703

2

3

4

5

MASANORI INUI

INUIINUI.COM · FACEBOOK.COM/INUIMASANORI

The forthcoming Holidays

Mixed media, digital media • Fiction

Japan • *Hyogo, 13 January 1983*

inuinum@yahoo.co.jp • 0081 9091135017

1 I CALL FOR WIND   2 HIDE-AND-SEEK   3 THE NIGHT WITH THE GIRL   4 SONG FOR THE JOY   5 COME ON EVERYBODY

1

HILLS - KOREA ILLUSTRATION SCHOOL
DIRECTOR: KWON HYEOKSOO
COORDINATOR: CHA SEUNGJA

4

MIHWA JEON

JEONMIHWA.TISTORY.COM

Raindrops patter • Poster colour on paper • Fiction

Republic of Korea • *Seoul, 5 January 1978*

2001agassi@hanmail.net • 0082 194096702

5

HILLS - KOREA ILLUSTRATION SCHOOL
DIRECTOR: KWON HYEOKSOO
COORDINATOR: CHA SEUNGJA

4

1

2

3

WON HEE JO

An important problem • Oil pastel, coloured pencils • Fiction

Republic of Korea • *Seoul, 18 March 1979*

sada2@naver.com • 0082 1090740746

"ASTRID THE FLY DISCOVERS MUSIC". BONNIER CARLSEN. STOCKHOLM. 2013
"ASTRID THE FLY LIKES". BONNIER CARLSEN. STOCKHOLM. 2013
"A WALK". BONNIER CARLSEN. STOCKHOLM. 2013
"ASTRID THE FLY RUNS AWAY". BONNIER CARLSEN. STOCKHOLM. 2010
"ZUCCHINI FOR A DACHSHUND". BONNIER CARLSEN. STOCKHOLM. 2009
"ASTRID THE FLY FLIES HIGH". BONNIER CARLSEN. STOCKHOLM. 2008
"KOLLA KROPPEN! RABEN&SJÖGREN". STOCKHOLM. 2008
"MORRIS HOS FRISÖREN". BONNIER CARLSEN. STOCKHOLM. 2007
"ASTRID THE FLY". BONNIER CARLSEN. STOCKHOLM. 2007
"MORRIS IN THE BIG MEADOW". BONNIER CARLSEN. STOCKHOLM. 2006
"MORRIS AND GRIFFO". BONNIER CARLSEN. STOCKHOLM. 2006
"MORRIS HAS A SWIM". BONNIER CARLSEN. STOCKHOLM. 2005
"REVOLTING". RABEN&SJÖGREN. STOCKHOLM. 2005
"KAJSA GILLAR". BONNIER CARLSEN. STOCKHOLM. 2003
"MORRIS PÅ MORGONEN". BONNIER CARLSEN. STOCKHOLM 2003
"MORRIS PASSAR HUSET". BONNIER CARLSEN. STOCKHOLM. 2002
"MORRIS OCH STRUMPAN". BONNIER CARLSEN. STOCKHOLM. 2002
"HUNDLIV". BONNIER CARLSEN. STOCKHOLM. 2001
"PIRATER OCH PRINSESSOR". BONNIER CARLSEN. STOCKHOLM. 2000
"PRATA PERSILJA". BONNIER CARLSEN. STOCKHOLM. 1999

1

3

5

1 IT WAS EVENING WHEN SHE CAME   2 GOODBYE. SHE SAID. THANKS FOR THE MILK   5 THEY LEFT IN THE MORNING
3 THE GRAY FOLLOWED THE GIRL'S TRAIL THROUGH THE WOODS

Flickan från långt borta (The girl from far away)

Watercolour and pigment liners • Fiction

Bonnier Carlsen, Stockholm, 2014, ISBN 9789163873348

Sweden • *Gävle, 22 February 1958*

maria.joensson@telia.com • 0046 705558869

MARIA JÖNSSON
SPYFLUGAN.COM

2

3

4

5

JUNAIDA

JUNAIDA.COM · INSTAGRAM.COM/JUNAIDA_IG

HOME • Watercolour, pencil • Fiction
Sunreed Co, 2013, ISBN 9784914985578
Japan • *Tokyo, 31 May 1978*
junaida55@yahoo.co.jp • 0081 09082337222

"ALJA DOBI ZAJČKA", CENTER ZA SLOVENSKO
KNJIŽEVNOST, LJUBLJANA, 2014
"DEŽELA BOMB, DEŽELA TRAV", CENTER ZA SLOVENSKO
KNJIŽEVNOST, LJUBLJANA, 2013

MAJA KASTELIC

MAJAKASTELIC.BLOGSPOT.COM

A Boy and a House

Watercolour • Fiction

Slovenia • *Novo Mesto, 25 September 1981*

maja.kastelic@gmail.com • 0038 641915114

"NEKKOBAA NO OKURIMONO". POPURASHA. TOKYO. 2012
"LITTLE RED RIDING HOOD". IWASAKI SHOTEN. TOKYO. 2012
"RAPUNZEL". IWASAKI SHOTEN. TOKYO. 2011
"NATSUNEKO". KODANSHA. TOKYO. 2011
"SHOGAKUSEI NI NARUHI". SHINNIHON SHUPPANSHA. TOKYO. 2010
"SNOW WHITE AND ROSE RED". IWASAKI SHOTEN. TOKYO. 2010
"CINDERELLA". IWASAKI SHOTEN. TOKYO.2009
"HANSEL AND GRETEL". IWASAKI SHOTEN. TOKYO. 2009
"SORA NO KI". IWASAKI SHOTEN. TOKYO. 2008
"RUU TO RINDEN". KODANSHA. TOKYO. 2008
"THUMBELINA". KAISEISHA. TOKYO. 2007
"LITTLE RETRO TRAM". RIRONSHA. TOKYO. 2007
"KANON". KODANSHA. TOKYO. 2006
"TAMARIN TO POCHIRO". KODANSHA. TOKYO. 2004
"SABOTEN". KODANSHA. TOKYO. 2002

2

3

4

1 TEENY-TINY KA-NYA THOUGHT TO HERSELF. "I THINK I'D LIKE TO TRY TO SLEEP IN THIS MATCHBOX! AND I'LL NEED A PILLOW TOO." SHE THEN PULLED SOMETHING SOFT FROM A NEARBY PLANT, AND SLIPPED INTO THE BOX FOR A LITTLE NAP   2 KA-NYA DECIDED TO GO OUT FOR A LITTLE ADVENTURE. SHE WAS OVERWHELMED BY HOW MANY FUN THINGS THERE WERE TO DO OUTSIDE. FIRST SHE DECIDED TO HOP ON THE TRAM   3 THE TRAM ENTERED A TUNNEL. INSIDE THE TUNNEL STARS WERE TWINKLING EVERYWHERE. KA-NYA SAW A MAMA BEAR AND HER CUBS POPPING STARS INTO THEIR MOUTHS. SHE DECIDED TO DO THE SAME. THEY TASTED LIKE ROCK CANDY   4 AT LAST THE TRAIN LEFT THE TUNNEL. SUDDENLY AN ENORMOUS CHILD APPEARED AND TOOK KA-NYA INTO THE PALM OF HER HAND. "IT'S TIME TO GO HOME NOW." AS KA-NYA RODE ON THE GIRL'S GIANT HAND THE TRAM AND THE RIVER SEEMED TO GET SMALLER. THE GIRL PLACED KA-NYA ON TOP OF AN OPEN BOOK. "THAT'S ALL FOR TODAY"   5 ONE BY ONE. KA-NYA. THE TRAM. THE MATCHBOX. AND ALL OF THE OTHER PLAYTHINGS WERE SWEPT INTO THE BOOK. WHEN THE LAST ONE HAD MADE IT INSIDE. THE GIRL'S ROOM WAS ONCE AGAIN SPOTLESS. "GOODNIGHT KA-NYA. SEE YOU TOMORROW"

5

YOKO KITAMI
ASAHI-NET.OR.JP/~BG4T-KTM

Matchibako no Ka-nya (Ka-nya in the Matchbox) · Oil painting · Fiction
Hakusensha Incorporated, Tokyo, 2013, ISBN 9784592761631
Japan · *Kamakura, 20 February 1957*
k-yoko@art.email.ne.jp · 0081 0333710148

"HLBOKOMORSKÉ ROZPRÁVKY". ARTFORUM. BRATISLAVA. 2013

BRATISLAVA ACADEMY OF FINE ARTS AND DESIGN
SCHOOL DIRECTOR: STANISLAV STANKOCI
COORDINATOR: DUŠAN KÀLLAY

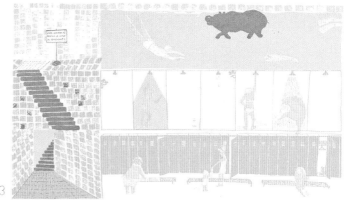

VERONIKA KLÍMOVÁ

VERONIKAKLIMOVA.SK

The swimming pool • Silk screen • Fiction

Slovakia • *Bratislava, 13 April 1989*

veronikaholecova@gmail.com • 00421 902164702

1

2

ECV ÉCOLE DE COMMUNICATION VISUELLE
SCHOOL DIRECTOR: SUZANNE HADDAD
COORDINATOR: MARIA FAURE

3

5

PAUL LAROCHE

CARGOCOLLECTIVE.COM/PAUL-LAROCHE
PAULLAROCHE.TUMBLR.COM

Moby Dick • Linocut • Fiction

France • *Villeneuve-Saint-Georges, 29 November 1994*

paul.lrch@gmail.com • 0033 0671168996

2

3

96

4

5

JI YEON LEE

Seoul, there • Painting • Non fiction

Republic of Korea • *Gyeongsangnam-do, 16 November 1977*

ji7158@naver.com • 0082 01085572663

1 WHERE DOES IT ALL GO? 2 WHAT DO YOU THINK? ISN'T IT SURPRISING? IT IS A NEW ISLAND ANYWAY 3 THIS IS HOW WE LIVE HERE. WE CAN DRESS UP IN OUR OWN WAY 4 SHIPS COME TO COLLECT TRASH SOMETIMES 5 PEOPLE STILL DO NOT KNOW ANYTHING. YET THE ISLAND IS GROWING BIGGER

2

3

4

5

MYEONG AE LEE

MYUNGAELEE.COM

Plastic Island · Ink, watercolour, mixed media · Non fiction

Sangbooks, Seoul, 2014, ISBN 978899112642877810

Republic of Korea · *Seoul, 05 October 1976*

reinvest@naver.com · **0082 1099754149**

How much can a rich visual culture, and in particular a "contemporary" visual culture, influence an illustrator's work?

As John Donne wrote, "No man is an island" I think that in today's hyperconnected world, it is nearly impossible for any artist to stay completely free of influence. From the moment we are born everything we see and every experience influence our way of creating and making. At the same time, each good illustrator brings a unique hand to his or her subject, and no two illustrators are ever exactly the same.

How is the diffusion of digital formats changing illustration?

The proliferation of tools, especially digital, for illustration gives artists myriad options to make, create, adjust, and alter their work. Skills with computer software and techniques can go a long way today. But I would like to believe that the emotional and intellectual qualities of a well-done work of illustration are hard to create with a computer alone. The artistry still has to be there.

Was there something (in terms of techniques, themes) that you expected to find among the works presented that you didn't find?

I fully expected to see much more work devoted to the pressing issues of today that children should be – and are – aware of, such as the environment and pollution. I saw dozens of retellings of *Little Red Riding Hood*, but nothing about what children can do for Mother Earth. I found that very discouraging.

Could you name some references to art history that you singled out among the submitted works?

I saw a wide variety of references, from the Peking opera *Farewell My Concubine* to the American TV show *The Simpsons*, and illustrations inspired by the work of Miró, Magritte, Duchamp, Picasso, Matisse, Warhol, and many, many more. Some of them were well done; but most of them were not chosen for the exhibition.

How do the laws of the market influence artists' ability to create stories?

In my opinion the laws of the market have a lot to do with the overall cultural politics of society, in terms of the official status of the child as well as of the

culture of children. In Sweden, the famous director of the Unga Klara children's theatre in Stockholm, Suzanne Osten, in a recent radio interview didn't hesitate to express her view that "racism against children exists in Sweden." The official objective is to honour and respect children, but when it comes to economic conditions for art, literature, theatre and film for children, this respect suddenly fades away. On one hand, there are a lot of gatekeepers who talk about what topics and formats children like and understand, protecting them from real life. On the other, children are hostages to raw commercialism.

In her 2007 PhD thesis, the Swedish economist Jenny Lantz described a phenomenon that tends to occur in medium-sized culture producing enterprises when emphasis moves from the traditional cultural pole to the economic pole, that is from an often silent knowledge of taste and quality in art (seen from the perspective of the public) to a discussion of a broad taste, mainstream and, in my opinion, a "quality of selling." Young marketing people, usually men, often claim that they have a professional relation to taste, that they themselves are objective and either can step out of their own taste, or that they share the taste of the wider public. They show, and are proud to feel, what they call professional enthusiasm towards their products.

Interesting enough, Lantz saw a clear tendency: when focus was laid on the economic pole, culture-producing firms risked going out of business in a span of a few years; I would say that in Sweden we are seeing the same developments in the book industry. Many of the bigger publishing houses have had to undergo painful structural reconstructions where economic views are taking over: more mainstream, more dead mass literature imports, few artistic highlights. A "more of the same" instead of looking for new signals.

Similarly, big bookshop chains are claiming that books have to sell themselves. They do more to give their clients more of the same – that being books that they have already read, books by very well known authors or books that are in the mainstream – than they do to help them to find new, more artistic or thematically challenging ones. Booksellers usually don't want to expand their views or be involved in debut and experimental books.

It is also a sad fact that the market wants self-selling picture books in two distinct age categories: 0-3 and 3-6 years. The second category has to house all picture books in what is now a rich and expanding range of books for other age categories, including adults – say 6-10, 10-13 and 13-90 years. To say that these market laws create confusion among adult buyers, finding all these expanding picture books in the 3-6 years piles, is an understatement!

This shows some of the structural conditions around creating new picture book stories. It is a risky project in Sweden.

Searching for new expressions and stories or coping with what already sells is a consideration for young Swedish artists wanting to establish themselves as creators of picture books today. It is a fact that each book must carry its own costs, that there is no time for maturing or developing their storytelling over time. It is a fact that very few publishers today are willing to build up authors, to accept minor successes or "in-between" books. That means that young artists often have to be entrepreneurs from the beginning. They need to come up with a selling concept at once, as well as merchandising plans. A common idea nowadays is to start an online shop as soon as possible.

The good news is that there are many pop-up small, experimental, one person publishers, daring to take risks and support brand new talent from art schools, as well as buying original and new books from abroad.

When it comes to developing new and original picture books, it seems that Norway has come up with a constructive support system to ensure the time needed to produce good, high quality picture books. A grant is shared between the publisher and the artist, and it has shown to be a true success story. The artist can try out their idea in advance, being judged by a qualified jury. The grant gives them enough time to carry out the project.

Should children's picture books tackle difficult issues, such as loss, death, illness and war?

Yes, indeed! Try asking the same question about adult literature.

I often quote the Danish dramatist and picture book author Oscar K. who maintains that everything can be told to a child, but serious topics can only be handled by great authors. It takes time to master those issues.

Most often I feel that there is a lack of artistic, emotionally powerful, daring and high-octane books featuring real life catastrophes like war, terrorist attacks, tsunamis, firestorms, ship and air wrecks and sudden death in families and societies. We cannot hide those sides of human life from children. How can we protect them from life itself? We have to tackle those issues, however painful they may be to us as adults. It is possible to explain and handle sorrow, but it gives rise to anxiety and trauma when it is unspoken or hidden. Children pick up on these things anyway, but we must show them enough respect to talk about it seriously. As adults, we think that books on these issues are too difficult for them to understand, but children never think that they don't understand. The fact is that they always understand, but always in their own way, and that's ok! So we can stop giving them the illusion that there is one accepted way of understanding existential issues like death, sorrow, joy, love and happiness: life itself.

We must not forget that children dwell, and that childhood itself is "performed," within or very close to "the border of chaos" and darkness, according to the Finnish brain specialist Matti Bergström. He describes the no-man's-land between the old brain (stem) and the not yet developed, logically structured "white world" of the new brain (neocortex) of adults. The child, still dominated by the emotional brain (the limbic system), is balancing the chaos of the "black world," playing sometimes dangerous games, having strong emotions and being capable of fierce creativity, setting it against the structured institutions of the adult, with their logically structured world and preferred "white" controlled games. Children have to express and share these border experiences with their adults, getting to know that darkness is normal like life itself, but that life is worth it, that creativity and imagination are worth it, and that there is hope for the future.

To meet the child in that no-man's-land area could mean telling stories that don't avoid talking about "life itself," and even telling stories from the gaze of the child itself, in a child-centric way. That means that the narrator is standing in the shoes of a child, expressing the world view (thoughts, feelings, emotions, vocabulary, syntax) within a child's cognitive frames. There is no adult narrative voice explaining things, clarifying the world, because children do not understand, or even know about, the adult way of understanding things, i.e. in any given, right way. You could say that it includes a poetic view of the world and a will to accept the poetic, artistic and aesthetic challenges of expressing your story from an empathetic, children's perspective in both image and text. Holding this narrative perspective, handling real-life topics in artistic, poetic, symbolical or imaginative ways can result in these multi-layered, enigmatic, high quality picture book stories, rich in subtext and of great, long-lasting artistic value.

One example of a difficult topic told from a child's perspective is by Maira Kalman who came up with the first, and up to now only, picture book about the 9/11 disaster, *Fireboat* (2002), which tells the story from the perspective of an old but very brave little fireboat, doing its best to help the world on that awful day.

The Indian book cooperative company Tara books seems to be the only publishing house that has come up with a book about the 2004 tsunami disaster, rich in colours, myth and symbols, showing survivors and victims in a big flooding river.

The Norwegian picture book creators, poet Gro Dahle and artist Svein Nyhus, have produced several books on serious topics – family violence, psychosis and alcoholism in families – breaking several taboos and giving children reference points to recognize from their own lives and surroundings, as well as possibilities of raising discussions with adults.

We do have some very good authors of children's novels and picture books in Sweden using the same perspective of telling stories to children, dealing with serious topics: Barbro Lindgren, Eva Eriksson, Anna-Clara Tidhom, Thomas Tidholm and Eva Lindström, among others. But, as yet, we do not have any picture books that deal with catastrophes. And none of the bigger publishing houses have ever shown any interest in the more complex picture books from abroad. Kalman does not exist in the Swedish book market yet, there are very few Tara books and, like the Dahle/Nyhus-books, they were brought to Sweden by very small publishers such as Hjulet (Tara books) and Daidalos (Dahle/Nyhus).

As a juror, is it difficult to judge the pictures outside of the context for which they were designed, that being the illustrated book?

Yes, it is! As a juror, it is not possible to judge the pictures without considering the context for which they were created.

In Sweden, there is an on-going discussion among illustrators if it is perhaps not time to distinguish between single pictures, or illustrations that relate to an idea, a concept or a given text (as in an illustrated tale, a text-based story or a short children's novel), and sequential pictures, like those in a picture book, that are narrating a story in the book, frequently alongside a text.

In either case, as a juror, your mission is to judge how the context is handled: in relation to what these pictures are "good?" A picture book, telling a story through both images and text, and most often structurally merging with the formal, technical and graphic medium of the book, has to be judged with respect to that overall system. Once merged that system is irreversible, neither the pictures nor the text or the very medium of the book itself could be taken apart!

Picture book images have double or even triple contexts when they are telling a story. They are dependent on the story itself (together with the text), but also dependent on the very text in the actual spread (the "text image") and on the other pictures in the sequence. As a juror, you have to study the amalgamation of the story, the dramaturgy of "the drama of the turning of the page," as Barbara Bader calls it, the quality of the paper, the graphic qualities of the *mise-en-page*, the distinct choice of typography, colours and painting techniques.

You cannot judge a single image from a picture book without taking these contexts into consideration, it is not fair.

So you need the book, if it is published, to be exhibited alongside the images on the wall; you need the text-images in the pictures to avoid experiencing "a bad composition" with lots of empty spaces. If you are shown only a part of the book, you will need, at the very least, a synopsis of the story. Would you ever judge a film based on some stills, without spoken language or music?

And if the book is not yet published, you need to have the synopsis as well as a storyboard, where the sketches show the flow of the story giving you an idea about the whole project. The target of this particular picture book art is to consider the book as a medium as well as an artistic object; sometimes you have to discuss its possibilities to fulfil its intention.

Without the possibilities of contextualising the different agents, you are judging an odd collection of styles, techniques and manners that tell you nothing about the narrative competences of the story, or its relation to the readers. Is the book aesthetically challenging enough for child readers? Is there a recognisable, empathetic child perspective in the story, or is it telling a story from a traditional omnipotent, often ironic narrative perspective?

As a juror you also have to ask the opposite, does this book already exist? In what respect does this very book contribute to or add values to the art of the picture book in a literary, artistic, thematic or aesthetic sense?

As the Norwegian poet/author Gro Dahle says to her picture book students in art school, "the book you are creating must be crucial, otherwise it is of no interest. So why is this story invaluable? Does it take us to a new place?."

And Dahle's best piece of advice for story writing is to "go where the fire is! Break stones! And then – break more stones!"

In the words of the Finnish picture book historian and critic Maria Laukka, you always have to conclude your judgement of a book with this question, "why, at all, has this book been printed?."

Are there still differences in terms of style, technique and imagery in the work of artists from different cultural areas or does illustration tend to be globalised and comply?

Of course there are international styles (as in the often mentioned, elegant Bologna art styles), commercial mainstream styles and different, vague national styles. Different cultures foster different traditions, handicrafts and tastes due to technical and economical conditions, as well the artists' educational backgrounds and the overall status of children in the different cultures. Are picture books given the space to be artistic and literary fiction, or are they meant to serve as moral education or nicely disguised schoolbooks?

When judging picture books as a jury member, a critic or a university lecturer, you always are more of an expert of what you have experienced on your own piece of the map. It is a matter of differentiation and habits, and it takes a lot of training to be able to really see and judge what you see from other cultures, if it is actually possible. As a western European from the northern countries I really have to get used to the different ways of expression in the arts, as well as the myths and themes in the delicate stories and pictures from the Arab world, as well as in Russian, African and Asian art. The cultural symbols are quite different, as are the principles of composition, drawing perspectives and decorating the page. And when it comes to picture books, certain countries have a long history of printing books in colour, while others are just beginning. And there is always a risk for beginners to study and imitate the most apparent, superfluous, commercial trends in those cultures where picture books hold a vital, commercial market.

Getting to know Tara Books has for me been a very important, eye-opening project for quite some years. It has been fascinating to follow their projects, which seek to support the many different cultures of painting and storytelling in the various Indian regions. It is a broad cultural project to promote pride among people, to see and be proud of their own traditional stories and myths, and to create modern storytelling by connecting ceremonial decorations of different Indian regions and cultures with new themes and topics.

It is interesting to realise that what you see as high culture in your own country perhaps is not seen as such in another context, picture books do not always travel easily! Many rebellious small main characters in Swedish picture books are made less self-confident, shyer, weaker and less free in a number of translations abroad. The naivety, the child centric ideals of Sweden, the often-simple styles do not always tell the same story elsewhere.

Funny enough, it also means that most Swedish picture book artists do not feel very comfortable on the international stage of picture book art.

4

5

3 IT HAD BEEN A COUPLE OF DAYS BEFORE THE WHITE CAT CAME BACK   4 AFTER CLEANING ALL DAY. SHE FEELS SO TIRED AND SOON FALLS ASLEEP   5 THE OLD LADY'S HOUSE IS NO LONGER WHITE AS SNOW. BUT SHE IS OK WITH THAT

YUNWOO LEE
BLOG.NAVER.COM/YOUEE17

An old lady and her white house • Pencil, watercolour, digital media • Fiction

Republic of Korea • *Seoul, 27 March 1976*

youee17@hanmail.net • 0082 1023877897

ÉCOLE ESTIENNE (ESAIG)
SCHOOL DIRECTOR: ARMELLE NOUIS
COORDINATOR: STÉPHANE SOULARUE

2

MATHILDE LEPRISÉ

MATHILDELEZ.TUMBLR.COM

Le Plongeur (The Diver) • Indian ink, watercolour • Fiction

France • *Paris, 2 March 1994*

mathilde.leprise@gmail.com • 0033 0788004261

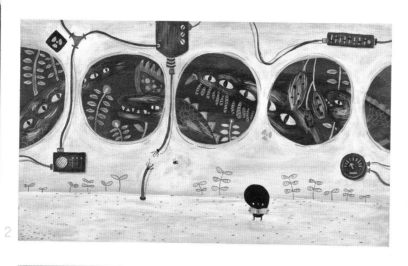

1 THE WORLD AFTER THE BOMB. AND ANIMALS ARE GROWING CONSTANTLY   2 I FOUND A RADIANT BUG THAT I HAVE NEVER SEEN

3 I TRY TO LOOK FOR ITS FRIENDS   4 BUT SOMEONE DISCOVERS US   5 EVERY MONSTER FOUND US

LIAN-EN LIN

BEHANCE.NET/NONESTATES · FACEBOOK.COM/NONESTATES

The Radiant Bug · Acrylic · Fiction

Taiwan · *New Taipei City, 14 November 1988*

xuo6p714@gmail.com · 0088 6953299311

HSU KUNG LIU

Whose stop is this? · Poster paint · Fiction

Hsin Yi Publications, Taiwan, 2013, ISBN 9789861614601

Taiwan · *5 October 1973*

susan@hsin-yi.org.tw · 00886 223965303 ext.1819

"LA MUJER MÀS ALTA DEL MUNDO". LIBRE ALBEDRÍO. SPAIN. 2014
"BESO". EL NARANJO EDICIONES. MÉXICO D.F.. 2014
"HANSEL Y GRETEL". OQO EDITORA. PONTEVEDRA. 2014
"PETITE CHOSE". ÉDITIONS AMATERRA. LYON. 2013
"YO SOY UN REFUGIADO". LOM EDICIONES (COLLECTIVE BOOK)
SANTIAGO. CHILE. 2013
"GLORIA FUERTES". HÉRCULES EDICIONES. A CORUÑA. 2013
"RAPUNCEL". OQO. PONTEVEDRA. 2012
"CALLE BLAS". EOLAS EDICIONES.(COLLECTIVE BOOK) LEON. 2012
"EL SEÑOR X". NARVAL EDITORES. MADRID. 2011

"JO M'EN VAIG". EDITORIAL CRUILLA (SM). BARCELONA. 2010

IRATXE LÓPEZ DE MUNÁIN

IRATXEDEMUNAIN.COM · FACEBOOK.COM/IRATXEILUSTRACION

Cuentos de Odesa (The Odessa tales) • Gouache and coloured pencils • Fiction

Nevsky Prospects, 2014, ISBN 9788494163760

Spain • *Pamplona, 31 May 1985*

iratxelopezdemunain@gmail.com • 0034 697676022

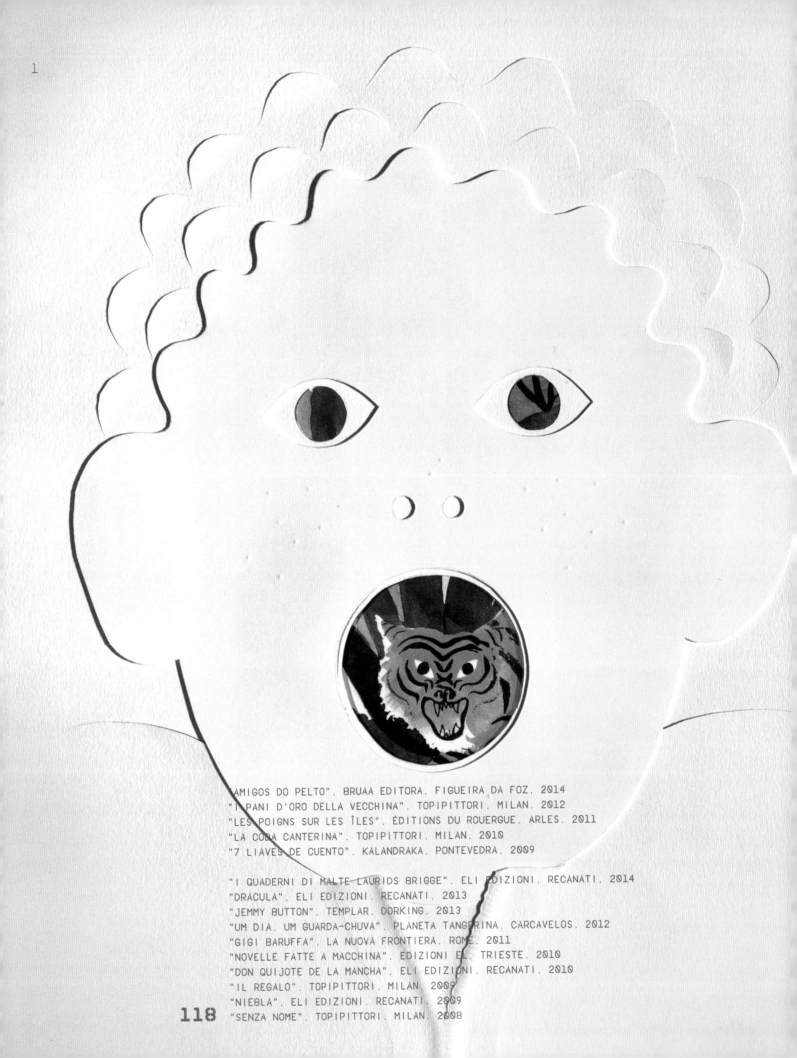

1

"AMIGOS DO PELTO", BRUAA EDITORA, FIGUEIRA DA FOZ, 2014
"I PANI D'ORO DELLA VECCHINA", TOPIPITTORI, MILAN, 2012
"LES POIGNS SUR LES ÎLES", ÉDITIONS DU ROUERGUE, ARLES, 2011
"LA CODA CANTERINA", TOPIPITTORI, MILAN, 2010
"7 LIAVES DE CUENTO", KALANDRAKA, PONTEVEDRA, 2009

"I QUADERNI DI MALTE LAURIDS BRIGGE", ELI EDIZIONI, RECANATI, 2014
"DRACULA", ELI EDIZIONI, RECANATI, 2013
"JEMMY BUTTON", TEMPLAR, DORKING, 2013
"UM DIA, UM GUARDA-CHUVA", PLANETA TANGERINA, CARCAVELOS, 2012
"GIGI BARUFFA", LA NUOVA FRONTIERA, ROME, 2011
"NOVELLE FATTE A MACCHINA", EDIZIONI EL, TRIESTE, 2010
"DON QUIJOTE DE LA MANCHA", ELI EDIZIONI, RECANATI, 2010
"IL REGALO", TOPIPITTORI, MILAN, 2009
"NIEBLA", ELI EDIZIONI, RECANATI, 2009
118 "SENZA NOME", TOPIPITTORI, MILAN, 2008

2

5

3

VIOLETA LOPIZ & VALERIO VIDALI

VIOLETALOPIZ.COM · FACEBOOK.COM/VIOLETA.LOPIZ   VALERIOVIDALI.COM · FACEBOOK.COM/VALERIO.VIDALI

The Forest · Inks, embossing, etching, paper cut · Fiction

Spain · *Ibiza, 19 December 1980*   **Italy** · *Lodi, 23 June 1983*

violopiz@yahoo.es · 0049 15204423437   valeriovidali@gmail.com · 0039 328 7322679

1 TREASURE: THE KING HAD ENORMOUS TREASURES, WHILE A WHITE HORSE WAS HIS FAVOURITE 2 CONSPIRACY: SEVEN KINGS CONSPIRED TO ATTACK THE BENARES 3 SIEGE: THE ENEMY BESIEGED THE CITY TIGHTLY 4 FIGHT BACK: THE GENERAL ON HIS WHITE HORSE DASHED FORWARD WHEN THE GATE OPENED 5 HOSTAGE: THE GENERAL CAPTURED ONE KING AND AT ONCE THE WHITE HORSE JUMPED ON ITS FEET AND FLIED BACK TO THE CITY

LING LUO

LUOLING.ARTP.CC

The White • Mixed media • Fiction

China • *Shanghai, 15 September 1981*

37250500@qq.com • 0086 13817900772

ÉCOLE EMILE COHL
SCHOOL DIRECTOR: PHILIPPE RIVIÈRE
COORDINATORS: FRÉDÉRIC MANSOT/ISABELLE CHATELLARD

JEOFFREY MAGELLAN

JEOFFREYMAGELLAN.TUMBLR.COM

Les copains (Friends)

Line drawings, digital media • Fiction

France • *Viriat, 24 December 1993*

jeoffreymagellan@yahoo.fr • 0033 0681028928

1

ACCADEMIA DI BELLE ARTI DI BOLOGNA
DIRECTOR: ENRICO FORNAROLI
COORDINATOR: LUIGI RAFFAELLI

2

3

4

5

5 SILENCE · 4 EMPTINESS · 3 ABUNDANCE · 2 KINDNESS · 1 LOSS

TERESA MANFERRARI

TERESAMANFERRARI.TUMBLR.COM
FACEBOOK.COM/TERESAILLUSTRAZIONE

La Venditrice di Parole (The Wordseller) · Acrylic · Fiction

Italy · *Gorizia, 16 July 1992*

teresamanferrari@hotmail.com · 0039 3485738968

ARS IN FABULA
SCHOOL DIRECTOR AND COORDINATOR: MAURO EVANGELISTA

4

MARCO MARINANGELI

BEHANCE.NET/FILICIO

Il leone buono (The Good Lion) – E. Hemingway

Pencil, watercolour • Fiction

Italy • *Fermo, 19 January 1990*

marco.marinangeli1990@gmail.com • 0039 3204146993

5 NEARBY MOON   4 CONTINOUS WAVE   3 UNKNOWN ISLAND   2 WARM ICEBERG   1 MOVING ROCK

MANUEL MARSOL

MANUELMARSOL.COM
MEDUSASYCEREBROS.BLOGSPOT.COM

Ahab and the White Whale
Watercolour, pencil, black ink, collage, oil, acrylic, digital media • Fiction
Edelvives, Madrid, 2014, ISBN 9788426394613

Spain • *Madrid, 28 April 1984*

manuelmarsol@gmail.com • 0034 676339483

"SHIKARAZUNI SUMU KOSODATE NO HINTO". GAKKEN. 2014
"OKAASAN HA ANATA WO INOCHIGAKEDEUMIMASHITA". SEISYUN PUBLISHING COMPANY. JAPAN. 2012
"SAIKARA HAJIMERU HANNYASINKYOU". FOREST PUBLISHING COMPANY. JAPAN. 2012
"KOKORONOSODACHI TO TAIWASURU HOIKU NO HON". GAKKEN. JAPAN. 2012
"BUDDA GA SENSEI". NAGAOKA. JAPAN. 2012

"KODOMO NO HATTATSU TO HOIKU NO HON". GAKKEN. JAPAN. 2011

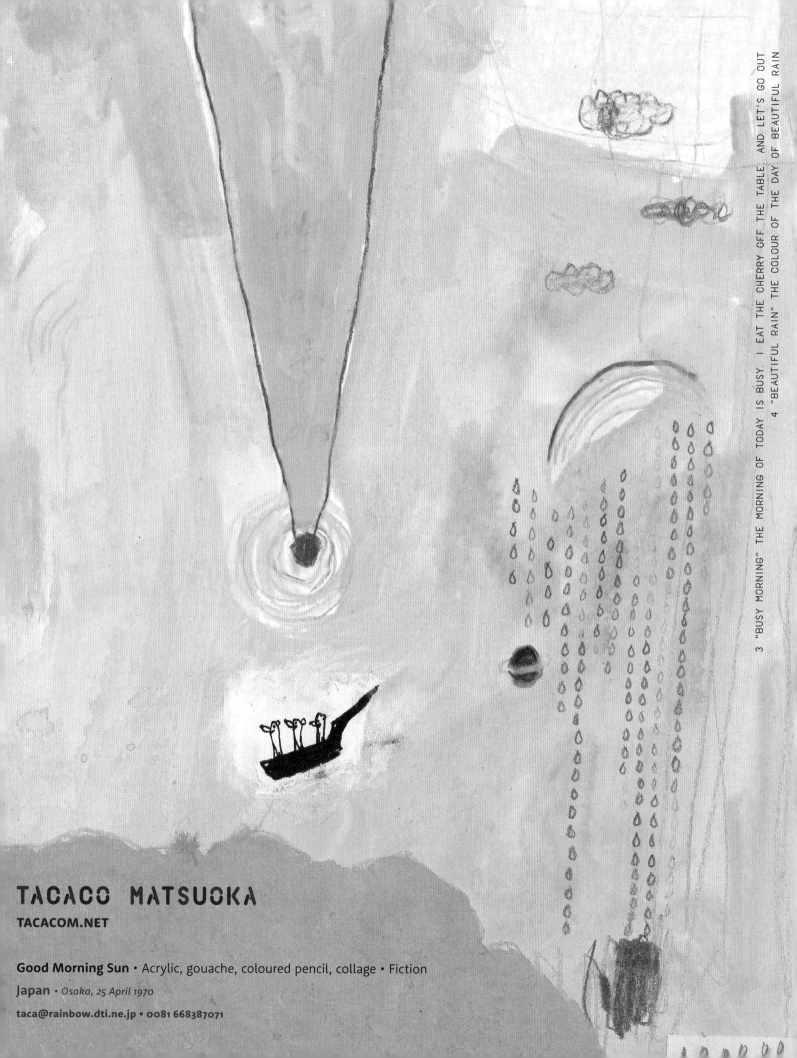

TACACO MATSUOKA
TACACOM.NET

Good Morning Sun • Acrylic, gouache, coloured pencil, collage • Fiction

Japan • *Osaka, 25 April 1970*

taca@rainbow.dti.ne.jp • 0081 668387071

3 "BUSY MORNING" THE MORNING OF TODAY IS BUSY. I EAT THE CHERRY OFF THE TABLE, AND LET'S GO OUT

4 "BEAUTIFUL RAIN" THE COLOUR OF THE DAY OF BEAUTIFUL RAIN

1 MYSTERIOUS PERFUME   3 THE FIRST DREAM. GO BACK TO THE PAST   4 THE SECOND DREAM. WHAT HAPPENS   5 THE THIRD DREAM IS JUST A DREAM

The Last Three Things • Pencil, digital media • Fiction

Taiwan • *Taoyuan, 29 January 1974*

hankhsu6@gmail.com • 00886 34896513

HSU MING HONG

FLICKR.COM/PHOTOS/SSHC

BEHANCE.NET/MINGHONGHSU

1 THE ROOSTER OPENED THE BOOK AND READ IT   2 THE ROOSTER OPENED THE BOOK AND READ IT AGAIN

3 "NICE IDEA!" EVERYONE AGREED WITH THE WOLF'S PROPOSAL   4 LASTLY. GOLDFINCH FLEW IN THE WOLF'S CHURCH.

HE COMES INTO A ROOM   5 WHAT DID THE WOLF DO AFTER THAT? HE NEVER EVER WANTED TO SEE GOLDFINCH

MAYA MIYAMA

MAYAMIYAMA.JIMDO.COM · MAYA-MIYAMA.TUMBLR.COM

The Wolf and the Goldfinch · Coloured pencils, pen, gouache · Fiction

Japan · *Tokyo, 19 November 1978*

maya1miyama@gmail.com · 0081 0422401601

1

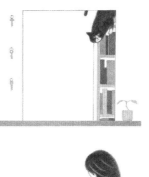

2

3

4

5

1 ONE DAY. WHEN GUYA WAS NOT PAYING ATTENTION WHILE READING HIS BOOK HE ACCIDENTALLY
DROPPED HIS BOOKMARK AND LOTTO GRABBED IT RIGHT AWAY AND THEN JUMPED UP TO THE TOP OF THE BOOKSHELF
2 GUYA THEN TRIED NEW THINGS THAT HE THOUGHT LOTTO WOULD LIKE BUT THERE WAS NOTHING THAT MADE LOTTO MOVE
3 AT THE END. GUYA HAD AN IDEA. HE WOULD GET A LADDER FROM THE GARAGE AND CLIMB UP THE BOOKSHELF
4 HOWEVER WHEN GUYA CAME BACK WITH THE LADDER HE REALIZED HE NO LONGER NEEDED IT   5 GUYA WENT BACK TO HIS READING

YEJIN MO

Sometimes it happens • Pencil on paper • Fiction

Republic of Korea • *Gyeonggi-do, 1 December 1985*

amu_mo@naver.com • 0082 10 56861201

"SINGING FOR THE MOTHERLAND". KANOON PUBLISHING
HOUSE. TEHRAN. 2012
"NO. I'M NOT AFRAID". BEHNASHR PUBLISHING HOUSE.
TEHRAN. 2009
"TRICK OF HEROES". BEHNASHR PUBLISHING HOUSE.
TEHRAN. 2007
"THE PRINCESS WHO COULD NOT LAUGH". KANOON
PUBLISHING HOUSE. TEHRAN. 2006

1 THE ENEMY IS ON THAT SIDE AND I AM ON THIS SIDE WITH MY SOLDIERS. WE ARE NOT SCARED OF TANKS AND GUNS 2 I GIVE THE ORDER TO ATTACK. THEN I HAVE PAIN IN MY LEG! 3 DADDY COMES AND CALLS ME FOR DINNER. MY UNCLE AND AUNTS KISS ME AND SAY: YOU SHOULD TAKE OFF YOUR LEG AT HOME 4 HE WONDERS WHEN HE SEES MY ARTIFICIAL LEG! I GIVE HIM MY LEG TO TRY AND I SHOUT CEASE FIRE. CEASE FIRE! 5 MY MOTHER SAYS FROM THE PHOTO FRAME. I AM PROUD OF YOU. GOOD NIGHT COMMANDER!

NARGES MOHAMMADI

NARGESMOHAMMADI.BLOGSPOT.COM

Good Night Commander

Collage, monoprint, pencil • Fiction

Ofogh Publishing House, Tehran, to be published

Iran • *Arak, 30 July 1978*

narsisus_moh@yahoo.com • 0098 9125476250

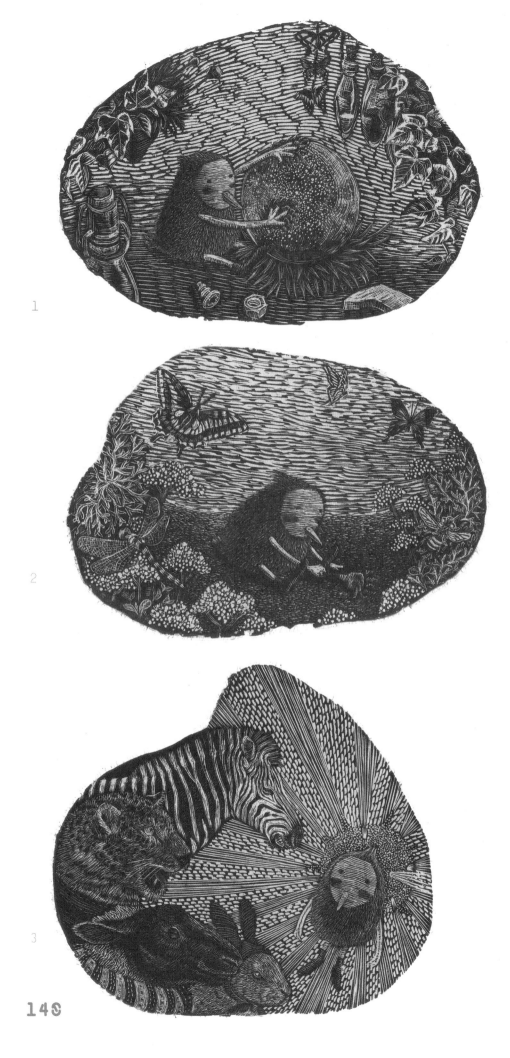

1

2

3

4

5

KAYOKO MORIYAMA

Star of Hojihoji kun • Wood engraving, watercolours • Fiction

Japan • *Aichi, 5 October 1966*

azukimaru11@icloud.com • 0081 0467396628

1   2   3

1 PE IS A LITTLE BOY WHO WANTS TO KNOW ABOUT THE WORLD SO HE GOES SEARCHING ABOUT LIFE   2 PE IS A BOY WHO HAS A KIND HEART AND HE MAKES COLOURFUL PAINTINGS   3 HE LOVES A POND WITH RED FISHES, HE IS DREAMING!   4 PE LOOKS AT THE MOUNTAIN. HE THINKS THAT THE MOUNTAIN IS LIKE AS A SLEEPING COW   5 PE IS SITTING ON A HILL AND HE IS LISTENING TO THE VOICE OF THE WIND

FERESHTEH NAJAFI

FERESHTEHNAJAFI.COM

Pe e o vasto mundo (Pe and the wide world) · Pastel and acrylic · Fiction

Editora Positivo, São Paulo, 2014, ISBN 9788538579021

Iran · *Tehran, 20 December 1974*

artinoos@yahoo.com · 0039 3457033332

1

HAW HAMBURG
SCHOOL DIRECTOR: DOROTHEA WENZEL
COORDINATOR: BERND MÖLCH TASSEL

2

4

5

3

NORA MARLEEN
NORAMARLEEN.DE

Fridobert and Carmen • Etching, aquatint • Non fiction

Germany • *Osnabrück, 24 April 1990*

norajanke@web.de • 0049 01737198147

1

1 THE HOUSE OF SILENCE   2 THE SQUARE OF STRANGE THINGS   3 THE SHOP WITH GOATS   5 THE HOUSE NEXT TO THE PARK

CLAUDIA PALMARUCCI

CLAUDIAPALMARUCCI.COM · CLAUDIAPALMARUCCI.BLOGSPOT.COM

On the way home • Oil and pencil on paper • Fiction

Italy • *Tolentino, 2 June 1985*

info@claudiapalmarucci.com • 0039 3921583161

1 TO HAVE TWO BODIES   2 WE WOULD LOVE EACH OTHER. SEEING FACE TO FACE.
3 TO HAVE THREE BODIES   4 ONE WOULD WORK AT HOME. ANOTHER GOES TO

DANCING THROUGH THE NIGHT WORK AND THE OTHER PLAYS OUTSIDE. EVERY EVENING WE WOULD COME BACK HOME AND TALK TOGETHER

SEKYOUNG PARK

BEHANCE.NET/SMILESEED

If I • Digital media • Fiction
Republic of Korea • *Seoul, 16 December 1974*
sekyoung1216@gmail.com • 0082 10 77323465

HAW HAMBURG
SCHOOL DIRECTOR: JACQUELINE OTTEN
COORDINATOR: BERND MÖLCK-TASSEL

1 ALLOTMENT GARDEN   2 COAT   3 TREE   4 MAN AND TIGER   5 MEETING IN A DREAM

NADINE PEDDE

NADINUSCHKA.TUMBLR.COM

Dreaming on the back of a tiger · Crayons on paper · Fiction

Germany · *Pritzwalk, 21 March 1986*

nadinuschka@gmx.de • 0049 017672972854

"RARO". EDELVIVES. MADRID. 2013

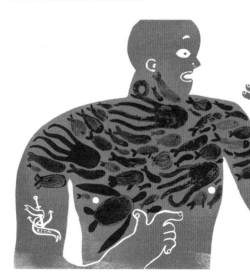

1 WILD BEASTS   2 THE DRAGON   3 ROBOTS AND ASTRONAUTS   4 THE FISHES FOLLOW   5 A BEAR

ANA PEZ
ANAPEZ.BLOGSPOT.COM

Mon petit frère invisible (My invisible little brother) • Ink and digital media • Fiction

L'Agrume Édition, Paris, 2014, ISBN 9791090743168

Spain • *Madrid, 30 January 1987*

ana.lapiz@gmail.com • 0034 628470918

"THAT'S WHAT I THINK. HOW ABOUT YOU?". KINERET PUBLISHING. TEL AVIV. 2014
"JACK AND DEATH". OQO EDITORA. PONTEVEDRA. 2013
"LA SIESTA DE LOS ENORMOS". OQO EDITORA. PONTEVEDRA. 2012
"FIVE PEAS FROM A POD". AGAWORLD PUBLISHING. SEOUL. 2010
"GALLO PINTO". OQO EDITORA. PONTEVEDRA. 2009
"JACK AND THE BEANSTALK". AGAWORLD PUBLISHING. SEOUL. 2008
"RUBY". MA PETIT CROKETTE. FRANCE. 2007
"WHAT DID THE SCARY WITCH ASK?". KEREN PUBLISHING. NEWARK. 2006
"THE FLY". KETER PUBLISHING. JERUSALEM. 2005

2

3

4

5

NATALIE PUDALOV

NATALIEPUDALOV.COM

Letters to Blue Dog • Mixed media • Fiction

Israel • *Nizny Novgorod, Russia, 5 September 1980*

p2natalie@yahoo.com • 00972 545509692

1 THE BALLOON MAN CROSSED THE MOUNTAINS   2 WHEN THE BALLOON MAN ARRIVES HE CALLS YOU FROM THE WINDOW BUT IN HIS OWN WAY BECAUSE HE IS A MAN OF FEW WORDS   3 HIS GIRLFRIEND CONTROLS THE TRUCK. A CALM QUEEN WHO KNOWS THE VALUE OF EACH SWEET   4 THE BALLOON MAN KNOWS EVERY CHILD IN EVERY TOWN AND CITY. THIS IS HIS SPECIAL TALENT AND HE KNOWS WHAT IS BEST FOR EACH ONE   5 HE KNOWS IT FROM THE MOMENT IN WHICH THE CHILDREN START WALKING. AS IF THERE WAS A NEW PATHWAY FOR THEIR FOOTSTEPS IN EVERY STREET. IN EVERY CITY. IN EVERY CROWD. IN EVERY COUNTRY

SIMONE REA

SIMONEREA.COM · SIMONEREA.BLOGSPOT.COM

L'uomo dei palloncini (The balloon man) · Pencil and crayon · Fiction

Topipittori, Milan, 2014, ISBN 9788898523146

Italy · *Albano Laziale, 27 November 1975*

simonerea@gmail.com · 0039 3493964483

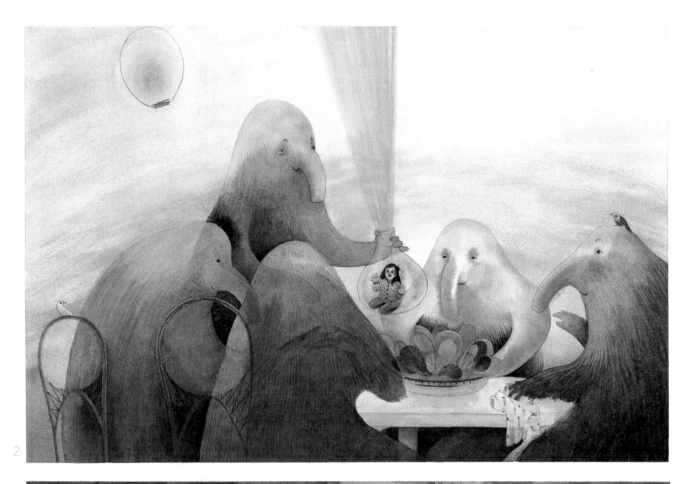

ARS IN FABULA
SCHOOL DIRECTOR AND COORDINATOR: MAURO EVANGELISTA

LEi

1 HER AND HER MOTHER (COVER) 2 DINNER WITH SIDE SALAD 4 WHEN IT IS TIME TO SLEEP

OLGA ROSA

ROSAOLGA.WORDPRESS.COM

Lei (Her) • Mixed media • Fiction

Italy • *Zevio, 28 December 1986*

olgarosa@hotmail.it • 0039 3408759459

1

HAW HAMBURG
SCHOOL DIRECTOR: JACQUELINE OTTEN
COORDINATOR: CHRISTIAN HAHN

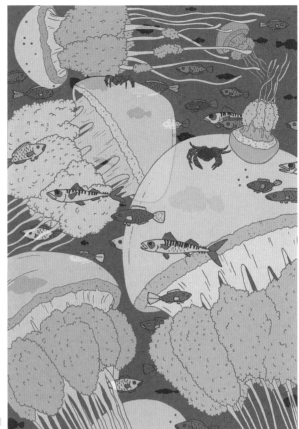

1 THE CLEANING SYMBIOSIS IN THE SEA   2 THE HERMIT CRAB AND THE SEA ANEMONE

3 THE CRAB AND THE JELLYFISH   4 THE PITCHER PLANT AND THE BAT   5 THE HORNBILL AND THE ZEBRA MONGOOSE

LENA KATHINKA SCHAFFER

LENASCHAFFER.DE

FACEBOOK.COM/LENASCHAFFERILLUSTRATION

Symbiosis in the Animal Kingdom · Ink and mixed media · Non fiction

Chile · *Santiago, 3 January 1987*

lenaschaffer@aol.com · 0049 15770605837

3

4

5

"UN DISFRAZ EQUIVOCADO". NÓRDICA. MADRID. 2015
"LA VOZ DEL ÀRBOL". ANAYA. MADRID. 2014
"LA PIEL EXTENSA". EDELVIVES. MADRID. 2013

162 "CAPERUCITA ROJA". NARVAL EDITORES. MADRID. 2011

THREE   4 FOUR   5 FIVE

ADOLFO SERRA

ADOLFOSERRA.BLOGSPOT.COM.ES

FACEBOOK.COM/ADOLFOSERRAILLUSTRATOR

The Journey · Acrylic, pencil, ink · Fiction

Spain · *Teruel, 31 August 1980*

serra.adolfo@gmail.com · 0034 606979857

CAMBRIDGE SCHOOL OF ART
SCHOOL DIRECTOR: CHRIS OWEN
COORDINATOR: MARTIN SALISBURY

2

3

THE TWO KARENS

& SUSAN

1 MISS CORR. KEEPER OF THE CANE   2 THE CLASS WATCHED IN SILENCE. GRATEFUL IT WASN'T THEM   3 "SUSAN! GET
TO THE TABLE... NOW!"   4 IT WAS THE TALK OF THE PLAYGROUND   5 SWIMMING LESSONS. INTRODUCING. THE TWO KARENS & SUSAN

MAISIE SHEARRING
MAISIEPARADISE.CO.UK · @MAISIEPARADISE

Susan's School Days. Stories from my Mum · Mixed media · Fiction

Great Britain · *Hull, 7 January 1991*

maisie.s@hotmail.com · 0044 07854835972

ÉCOLE NATIONALE
SUPÉRIEURE DES ARTS
DÉCORATIFS, PARIS
SCHOOL DIRECTOR: MARC PARTOUCHE
166 COORDINATOR: XAVIER PANGAUD

MARIE YAÉ SUEMATSU

MARIE-YAE.TUMBLR.COM

Waiting rooms · Pastel · Non fiction

France · *Paris, 7 November 1992*

marieyaesuematsu@hotmail.fr · 0033 06 67281500

1 LAST AUTUMN 2 LAST WINTER 3 THIS SPRING 4 THIS SUMMER 5 THIS AUTUMN

My Town • Digital media • Fiction

Japan • *Saitama, 17 October 1981*

mail@ryotakemasa.com • 0081 80 50803171

RYO TAKEMASA

RYOTAKEMASA.COM

FACEBOOK.COM/TAKEMASARYO

CHIHIRO TAKEUCHI

WEB-EHON.JP

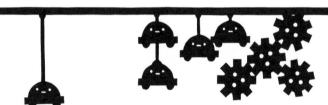

1 ONE MORNING. THE HAND WAS GONE

4-5 NOT EVEN HERE

Where is my hand?

Paper cutting • Fiction

Japan • *Hirakata City, 15 February 1971*

Y1100023@nifty.ne.jp • 0081 072 8982564

2

3

4

5

ELISA TALENTINO

ELISATALENTINO.IT · FACEBOOK.COM/ELISA.TALENTINO

Le Jardin d'Hiver (The winter garden) • Serigraphy • Non fiction

Print About Me Micropress, Turin, 2013

Italy • *Ivrea, 8 December 1981*

info@elisatalentino.it • 0039 3471083576

"CHONMAGE KACHO". SHUFU TO SEIKATSU SYA CO. TOKYO. 2007
"MOLEY". WANI BOOKS CO. TOKYO. 2007

U-SUKE

U-SUKE.CSIDE1.JP

Kuroton • Digital media • Fiction

Japan • *Yokkaichi City Mie, 11 December 1970*

atom7oy@aol.com • **0081 9091545945**

2

3

4

5

"EL LENGUAJE DE LOS ARBOLES". FINEO. MEXICO D.F., 2014
"MÉNAGE À DEUX". TUNNELLINGP. ROME. 2014
"LES FRAISES SAUVAGES". LIRABELLE. 2014
"JE M'EN VAIS". TUNNELLINGP. ROME. 2013
176 "ESTELA, GRITA MUY FUERTE!". FINEO. MADRID. 2008

1

Tous Les Soirs (Every evening) • Charcoal • Fiction

Italy • *Rome, 20 March 1978*

martina@martinavanda.com • 0039 3337817283

2

3

4

5

1 BIZARRE WIND LEAPING THROUGH THE TREETOPS. THE LITTLE BLACK BIRD IS REALLY FLYING
2 HERE IS SO DIFFERENT   3 THEY FEEL SAFER THAN THEY DO IN THE DARK NIGHT
4 GOOD NIGHT! I USED TO SLEEP IN THE BED ON THE GRASS   5 IN THE MISTY MORNING THEY GO OUT TO FIND FOOD

SHU-MAN WANG
FLICKR.COM/PHOTOS/AMANNWANG

Star Birds • Digital media • Fiction

Taiwan • *Taichung City, 17 October 1979*

aman1017@yahoo.com.tw • 00886 426230675

SATOKO WATANABE

SATOKO-W.COM · FACEBOOK.COM/SATOKO.ART

Story of A · Pencil, coloured pencils, Japanese paper · Fiction

Japan · *Kyoto, 12 January 1961*

sato@w.email.ne.jp · 0081 09031447573

3

"GODDAGDYR & GODNATDYR". GORILLAFORLAG. KØBENHAVN. 2014
"SNOTNÆSEN". TURBINE. AARHUS. 2014
"123". KLEMATIS. RISSKOV. 2013
"ABC". KLEMATIS. RISSKOV. 2013

123 og Abc (123 and Abc) • Watercolour, acrylic, markers, gouache • Fiction

Klematis, 2013, ISBN 9788764108552

Denmark • *Glostrup, 2 December 1975*

kamilla@tankestreger.com • 0045 25275005

KAMILLA WICHMANN
TANKESTREGER.COM

2

3

4

5

1 BLUE WAVE IS A BLUE HORSE THAT HAS BEEN TRAINED ONLY FOR THE WAR SINCE HE WAS BORN. HE IS STANDING ON A BATTLEFIELD WAITING FOR HIS FIRST WAR   2 THE MILITARY MAKES HIM GO AHEAD AND TAKES UP A LOT OF LANDS UNDERGOING THE ENDLESS WAR   3 AN OLD SOLDIER IS RUBBING CHARCOAL POWDER ON THE BODY OF BLUE WAVE TO RESCUE HIM   4 THE OLD SOLDIER LETS BLUE WAVE MOISTEN HIS THROAT AT A BIG RIVER THAT THEY REACHED WHILE WANDERING TO FIND A PLACE TO REST   5 HE CROSSES THE RIVER TO RESCUE A FAMILY IN DANGER. THEN THE CALM RIVER BEGINS TO WAVE WITH HIS STRUGGLE

JUNJAE YOO

The Blue Wave · Scratch on paper, digital media, acrylic, Korean ink · Fiction
Munhakdongne Publishing Group, Seoul, 2014, ISBN 9788954625753
Republic of Korea · *Seoul, 4 February 1976*
jjun2o4@hanmail.net · 0082 231443241

jjun2o4@hanmail.net · 0082 231443241

Re Tigre (King tiger) • Silk screen • Fiction

Orecchio Acerbo Editore + Else, Rome, 2014, ISBN 9788896806876

USA • *Seoul, Republic of Korea, 21 February 1989*

jooheeyoon@gmail.com • 01 9788283427

JOOHEE YOON

JOOHEEYOON.COM

JOOHEEYOON.TUMBLR.COM

1

4

3

5

1 THE KING WAS A BIG HERO IN ANCIENT TIMES   3 SOLDIERS ASKED THE KING TO KILL HIS WIFE BECAUSE THEY THOUGHT HIS WIFE CAUSED THEM TO LOSE THE WAR   4 HIS WIFE CHOSE TO COMMIT SUICIDE FOR HIM   5 IT WAS THE END OF AN ERA, AND IT LEFT NOTHING BUT THE KING'S HORSE

SHUAI YUE

Farewell my concubine • Propylene, traditional Chinese painting • Non Fiction

China • *Shandong, 4 August 1982*

40019671@qq.com • 0086 18878787801

GOOD BOOKS PROMOTE INTROSPECTION AND THE MYSTERIES OF EVERYTHING THAT IS ORDINARY

MILTON GLASER is among the most celebrated graphic designers in the world. He has had the distinction of one-man-shows at the Museum of Modern Art and the Georges Pompidou Center. In 2009, he was the first graphic designer to receive the National Medal of the Arts award. As a Fulbright scholar, Glaser studied with the painter Giorgio Morandi in Bologna, and is an articulate spokesman for the ethical practice of design. During his long and accomplished career, Glaser has also had the opportunity to come into contact with the world of illustrated children's books with *If Apples Had Teeth* (1960) and *The Alphazeds* (2003), created together with his wife Shirley Glaser.

What is the biggest challenge faced by someone who wants to tell a story through images?

First is to organize the imagery into a narrative that carries a story, without confusing the reader. This is called "low-level professionalism" and it is not necessarily a goal that I would personally search for. The other part of the challenge is to produce a work whose poetic content amplifies/extends the story itself into a symbolic experience that moves the mind.

How is creating images for children different to creating images for adults?

I have only a vague response to this cosmic question. I would assume that the innocence of children enables them to experience the world with less expectation and beliefs than adults have acquired. As a result, ideally at least, they are more open-minded and willing to accept ambiguity. Adults come to every experience already convinced that they understand the world. This is a great impediment.

Thinking beyond different styles and approaches, what are the characteristics that you think good illustrations for children's books ought to have?

Not to be repetitive, but a good book for children opens the mind to the possibilities that exist in life. Good books promote introspection and the mysteries of everything that is ordinary.

First published in the United States of America in 2015
by Chronicle Books LLC.

Originally published in Italy in 2015 by Maurizio
Corraini s.r.l.

ILLUSTRATORS ANNUAL 2015

© 2015 BOLOGNAFIERE & CORRAINI EDIZIONI
for the Publication

© 2015
BENJAMIN CHAUD
SVJETLAN JUNAKOVIĆ
CHARLES KIM
PAOLA PARAZZOLI
ULLA RHEDIN
for the jury report and the interviews

© ROGER MELLO
for the cover illustrations and the interview

© MILTON GLASER
for the interview

Book design
PIETRO CORRAINI
& CORRAINISTUDIO

Translations
ANTONELLA CESARINI
STEPHANIE JOHNSON
DAVID KELLY
ALESSANDRA MAESTRINI
GABRIELLA VERDI

Photographs
PASQUALE MINOPOLI

Image processing
MAISTRI FOTOLITO, VERONA

ISBN 978-1-4521-5439-8

Library of Congress Cataloging-in-Publication Data available.

Manufactured in China.

Interior design by Pietro Corraini & corrainiStudio.
Cover design by Roger Mello and Ryan Hayes.
Typeset in ARGN & Rooney.

10 9 8 7 6 5 4 3 2 1

CHRONICLE BOOKS LLC
680 SECOND STREET
SAN FRANCISCO, CA 94107

CHRONICLE BOOKS—we see things differently. Become
part of our community at www.chroniclebooks.com.